AF363338

SUFISM REVIVED

SUFISM REVIVED

A Contemporary Treatise on Divine Light,
Prophecy and Sainthood

By the Moroccan Sufi Master
SHAYKH MOHAMED FAOUZI AL-KARKARI

Translated by **YOUSEF CASEWIT**, Ph.D.
Edited by **KHALID WILLIAMS & TAREK GHANEM**

L·⌐ **LES 7 LECTURES**

Sufism Revived is published by the nonprofit organization
Anwar and his publishing house **Les 7 Lectures**

44, Fernand Brunfaut Street
1080 Brussels, Belgium

© Les 7 Lectures, 2021
All rights reserved

Cover Image: Don Fontijn

ISBN: 978-2-930978-52-9
Deposit number: D/2021/14.291/02 (Belgium)
Legal Deposit: February 2021

Table of Contents

SECTION I: PROPHETHOOD

1. Everlasting Intimacy (*Ulfat al-Khulūd*) 17

2. The Great Tiding (*al-Naba' al-ʿAẓīm*) 29

3. The Perfected Soul and the Partial Souls
(*al-Nafs al-kāmila wa'l-nufūs al-juzʾīya*) 39

4. The Father of Spirits 47

5. God Created him in His Image
(*Khalaqahu Allāh ʿalā Ṣūratihi*) 55

6. Sanctity is the Gate of Prophethood
(*al-Wilāya Bāb al-Nubūwa*) 67

7. The First Intellect (*al-ʿAql al-Awwal*) 79

SECTION II: MESSENGERHOOD

8. The Messenger and the Messenger of the Messenger
(*al-Rasūl wa-Rasūl al-Rasūl*) 93

9. The Station of Conveying the Message
(*Maqām al-Tablīgh*) 103

10. The Dialogue of the Names (*Ḥiwār al-Asmā'*) 117

11. The Mortal Human Nature of the Messenger
(*Basharīyat al-Rasūl*) 127

12. No god but God is the Key of Existence
(*Lā Ilāha illā Allāh Miftāḥ al-Wujūd*) 133

13. The *Alif* is the Foundation of the Levels of Religion
(*al-Alif Aṣl Marātib al-Dīn*) 141

SECTION III: SAINTHOOD

14. The Saint is the Treasure (*al-Walī Huwa al-Kanz*) 151

15. The Sainthood of Faith and the Sainthood of Gnosis
    (*Wilāyat al-Īmān wa-Wilāyat al-ʿIrfān*)............................. 159

16. I Become His Seeing (*Kuntu Baṣarahu*) 171

17. I Become His Hearing (*Kuntu Samʿahu*) 183

18. I Become His Hand (*Kuntu Yadahu*) 193

19. I Become His Foot (*Kuntu Qadamahu*)............................ 205

20. Adam's Image (*Ṣūrat* Adam ﷺ).. 215

21. He Who Knows Himself Knows His Lord
    (*Man ʿArafa Nafsahu ʿArafa Rabbahu*)............................. 223

22. The Assumption of Character Traits and the
    Verification of Truth (*al-Takhalluq wa'l-Taḥaqquq*)...... 229

23. Each Acts According to His Own Disposition
    (*Kullun Yaʿmal ʿalā Shākilatih*) 241

24. The Exclusive Oneness of the All and the Allness
    of Exclusive Oneness (*Majmūʿ al-Aḥadīya wa-Aḥadīyat
    al-Jumūʿ*)... 249

Conclusion 257

Works Cited 259

Index of Names & Terms... 263

أعوذ بالله من الشيطان الرجيم

بسم الله الرحمن الرحيم

بسم الله الرحمن الرحيم

بسم الله الرحمن الرحيم

بسم الله

بسم الله

بسم الله

الله

الله

الله

ولا حول ولا قوة إلا بالله العلي العظيم

Introduction

All praise belongs to You, dear God. You are the Light of the heavens and the earth. You bless, bestow, and provide. All favor is due to You until You are pleased.

To proceed: I received this book from myself by way of the spirit's allusion, and forged its meanings in a manner that can be conveyed through verbal expression, hoping that it may be a glad tiding for wayfarers. For it describes the waystations of realization that travelers will encounter on the Path, when they embark upon the vessel of direct witnessing within the soul and upon the horizons, until they join the ranks of the knowers of God who are absent from themselves and subsist through God. Such are the true knowers and the genuine sages.

There is a type of knowledge that is acquired by using the intellect, and another that comes by bestowal through opening the door of direct taste within the heart. Whoever wants to know through direct taste must gain it on its own terms, for every kind of knowledge must be taken from where it is found. As for the one who denies direct taste, he is saying that the religion is a body without a spirit. A person must adopt an attitude of resignation regarding everything that he does not know, and must act upon what he does know, so that he may receive from

God what was once hidden from him. For denial is the harbinger of spiritual deprivation, while active affirmation is the celestial steed of divine success. May God have mercy upon a servant who beholds what my pen inscribes with fair judgment, and puts aside what his intellect does not grasp, in the hopes that he may be given the grace to apply its teachings to his own character.

In this book, the disciple will find support in his journey toward the *Alif* through the *Hā'*-sphere. The Everlasting Presence (*ḥaḍrat al-khulūd*) takes on three aspects: the aspect of Prophethood (*nubuwwa*), the aspect of Messengerhood, (*risāla*), and the aspect of Sainthood (*wilāya*). In it, the disciple learns how to imbibe from the Spring of Prophethood, drink from the Niche of Messengerhood, and witness from the Lamp of Sainthood. I endeavored to bring all of this together in a smooth style that is perfumed with the Light of truth; and it is God who gives success.[1]

---

1   The original Arabic title of this book is *Afānīn al-Sujūd li-Alif al-Khulūd* ("The Arts of Prostration of the Eternal Alif"). It was first published by Maṭbaʿat Ṣināʿat al-Kitāb (Casablanca, 2017). The present English translation was made possible through the generous support of Saif Islam, El Mehdi Amine Boutayeb, Saad Ansari, Maham Haq, Ramzi Taleb, and Afifa Rahman.

SECTION I
PROPHETHOOD

1.

Everlasting Intimacy
(*Ulfat al-Khulūd*)

Mudhākara from the Friday
Gathering of 28th Muḥarram 1436/21st November 2014

Bismillāh al-Raḥmān al-Raḥīm

Know, may God illuminate your heart with the Light of His sanctity, that we shall speak about the Presence of the Prophets in a general fashion. As such, these lessons will serve as summaries, as it were, of all the Prophets. We shall address their being at the Station of the *Alif* through a *Hā'*-reading of the divine name.[2] Moreover, given that the *Alif* is composed of three principal dots that are vertically aligned, the upper part is specific to the presence of the messengerhood (*risāla*), the lower part

---

2   Translator's note: In the Shaykh's writings, the *Hā'* is the first of seven readings of the divine Name *Allāh*. It is followed by the *Lām* of Constriction (*lām al-qabḍ*) or of Love (*lām al-'ishq*), the *Lām* of Gnosis (*lām al-ma'rifa*), Separation (*faṣl*), Union (*waṣl*), the Hidden *Alif* (*al-Alif al-muqaddar*), and the Treasure-Dot (*al-nuqṭa al-kanzīya*). In the first reading of the divine name, i.e., a reading of the name Allāh as *Hū*, meaning 'He,' the disciple learns to behold all things as disclosures of God's names and qualities, in anticipation of entrance upon the *Lām* of Love.

to the presence of prophethood (*nubūwa*), and the middle dot to the liminality of sainthood (*barzakhīyat al-wilāya*). As such, every Prophet is necessarily a saint, but not every saint is a Prophet. When I say that the *Alif* has an "upper" and a "lower" part, this is only by way of illustration. But the problem with an illustration is that it gives an impression of spatial direction on paper.

Thus, in order to approximate the realities of wayfaring through the levels of the Name, we say through the Lord's assistance, that the wayfarer's journey begins by reading the levels of the Name experientially. He enters into the *Hā'* of Identity (*Hā' al-huwīya*) by struggling against the lower self until he passes away from it and from everything other-than-God. The subtle grace of the innermost secret that flows through every existent then manifests itself, and the wayfarer comes to naught in the Lights of *Hū*. When he becomes established in this station, the sun of the *Lām* of Constriction (*lām al-qabḍ*) shines upon him till its rays reveal the reality of the center of the divine entity. For it is from this center that the circle of the *Hā'* is configured, and through it that it is manifested. His heart does not look away from this sun, and he is overpowered by the assault of *Lahū*, 'for Him.' This sun becomes the *qibla* of his spirit and his heart. Then the pure meanings of the *Lām* of Gnosis manifest themselves to him through his arrival at the substantial reality of extinction in love and yearning. He then returns "to God" (*Lām-Lām-Hā'*, *lillāh*), breathing the fragrance of **to God we belong and to Him we return** (*innā lillāh wa-innā ilayhi* *rājiʿūn*).[3] When the wayfarer gains firmness in this station, and understands the pure meanings, celestial realities, and divine disclosures of "to God" (*lillāh*), then the banners of union are raised for him and he is cast into the ocean of the names of beauty till he becomes joyful and happy, and then returns to the ocean of separation where he experiences the realities of the names of majesty. For the genuine servant must discover the Real in majesty and in beauty until his circle of gnosis (*maʿrifa*) reaches its perfection.

Similarly, the wayfarer should search for union in the very kernel of separation. For the knower of God is the one who discovers life in the heart of death; and when he discovers union in separation, he penetrates into the liminal reality of sainthood where he comes into contact with the *Alif*. At that point, he may genuinely seek the replenishing subtle graces (*raqāʾiq*) of the Prophets. The blessed Messenger of God ﷺ said: "'The earth is never devoid of forty men who are like the intimate friend of the All-Merciful (*khalīl al-Raḥmān*). It is through them that others are given rain and granted assistance. Whenever one of them dies, God substitutes another one in his place.' Qatāda said: 'We have no doubt that al-Ḥasan [b. ʿAlī] is one of them.'"[4]

---

3   Q Baqara 2:156. The Qurʾān translations in this book are from *The Study Quran*, with occasional modifications.

4   Ṭabarānī, *al-Muʿjam al-awsaṭ*, 4:247.

There is another hadith that confirms this meaning. It is transmitted by 'Abdullāh b. Mas'ūd ❧ who said:

"God's Messenger ❧ said: 'To God belong three-hundred hearts among His creatures that are upon the heart of Adam ﷵ; and to God belong forty hearts among His creatures that are upon the heart of Moses ﷵ; and to God belong seven hearts among His creatures that are upon the heart of Abraham ﷵ; and to God belong five hearts among His creatures that are upon the heart of Gabriel ﷵ; and to God belong three hearts among His creatures that are upon the heart of Michael ﷵ; and to God belongs one heart among His creatures that is upon the heart of Raphael ﷵ. Whenever the latter dies, God substitutes in his place one of the three; and when one of those three die, God substitutes in his place one of the five; and when one of those five dies, God substitutes in his place one of the seven; and when one of those seven dies, God substitutes in his place one of the forty; and when one of those forty dies, God substitutes in his place one of the three-hundred; and when one of those three-hundred dies, God substitutes in his place one of the common believers. It is through them that He gives life and death, sends down rain, causes plants to grow, and repels tribulations.'" 'Abdullāh b. Mas'ūd was asked: "How does He give life and death through them?" He responded: "Because they ask God to multiply their communities, and they multiply; they pray against tyrants, and the tyrants are brought down; they supplicate for rain, and rain is sent down; they ask for the earth to burst forth with plants, and it does; and when they supplicate, He repels all manner of tribulations through them."[5]

Prophethood, for its part, is a lordly function that the Almighty entrusts to whomever He wishes among His servants. It is God's sheer election and choice: He elects whomever He wishes among His servants and sends them to the people in order to rectify and guide them upon the Path of divine proximity and right guidance. A Prophet, moreover, is sent to confirm a previously revealed Law and to act upon it. He is divinely protected from minor and major sins, and commits no errors prior to or after prophethood. We must not imagine, therefore, that Moses ﷺ committed a grave sin (*kabīra*) when he killed the Egyptian. For this has an esoteric interpretation that is beyond the realm of your comprehension. Indeed, God said concerning him: **I have fashioned thee for Myself.**[6]

Furthermore, God endows Prophets with a supreme intellect. He perfects their character, disposition, and outward bodily form, and so they avoid sin by virtue of their perfected intellects. Thus He singles them out for protection from error, in contrast to all other human beings. God also endows Prophets with a Pleasing Soul (*nafs rāḍiya*) that is inundated by His good-pleasure. How then could they err? If an error were ascribed to a Prophet, then he would have to defer to another person who is better than him, which cannot be, since the Prophet defers in all matters to God alone.

5   Ibn 'Asākir, *Tārikh madīnat Dimashq*, 1:303-304.
6   Q Ṭāhā 20:41.

As for what has reached us in reports that ascribe sin to prophets, those are merely forms of disobedience, not the reality of disobedience (*maʿṣiya*). Every Prophet has an intellect that is specific to him, to his era, and to the people to whom he was sent. In other words, he has an intellect that encompasses the people of his era. In contrast, the intellect of Sayyidunā Muḥammad ﷺ is all-encompassing and universal. To this effect, Abū Hurayra ؓ said: "The Prophet ﷺ was asked: 'When did you become a prophet?' He replied: 'When Adam was still between spirit and body.'"[7] As such, the blessed Prophet ﷺ possesses the primacy and ultimacy of prophethood. Muslim also relates in his *Ṣaḥīḥ* that the blessed Messenger of God said: "I was given superiority over the Prophets on account of six: I was granted the all-encompassing words; I was granted victory through fear; war spoils were made permissible for me; the earth was made as a place of prostration and a source of ritual purity for me; I was sent to the entirety of mankind; and I was made the Seal of Prophets."[8] Thus, the circle of prophethood came to its completion through him, and he is its noble ringstone.

Moreover, the station of prophethood necessarily follows the station of messengerhood and draws from it. This is why we say that the dot of prophethood occupies the bottom of the *Alif,* while the dot of messengerhood occupies its upper part. Divine replenishment therefore descends upon the presence of

7   Tirmidhī, *Sunan*, 2:924.
8   Muslim, *Ṣaḥīḥ*, 1:210.

prophethood from the dot of messengerhood, for the message's circle of mercy is immense.

God says: **And We sent thee not, save as a mercy (raḥmatan) unto the worlds.**[9] The letter *tā'* of *Raḥmatan* is a connected-*tā'* (*marbūṭa* ة) not an open-*tā'* (*maftūḥa* ت), and that is a spiritual allusion to the all-encompassing circle of God's mercy unto the worlds. This explains why it is befitting for the verse to be part of the Chapter of the Prophets (*al-Anbiyā'*), for the Prophets were among the manifestation-sites of this message of mercy during their times.

Given that the presence of prophethood is subordinate to the presence of the messengerhood, God's folk deduced an important principle in spiritual training (*qā'ida tarbawīya*), namely that as long as the disciple is under the tutelage of his Shaykh, he is subordinate to him, draws from him, and follows his tracks. The disciple cannot surpass the station of his Shaykh until the Shaykh returns his Lord. To this effect, the Shaykh of our Shaykhs, Sayyidī Aḥmad b. ʿAlīwa (d. 1934) says in a poem:

After the death of the Shaykh, one who is like him appears.
For this is God's wont, and it does not change.

You should also know, dear wayfarer, that the non-delimited intellect of a Prophet differs from the delimited intellect of a human being. For it stems from the Primordial Origin (*al-mab-*

---

9   Q Anbiyā' 21:107.

da' al-awwal). In other words, it stems from prophethood's very first point of origin: the primordial beginning of knowledge. As such, prophetic knowledge returns vanishing things back to their source so that their concealed secrets and primordial roots are understood. This presence is therefore called the Everlasting Station (*maqām al-khulūd*), for Prophets possess the everlasting life of the Hidden *Alif*. As such, a Prophet remains a Prophet even if no one follows him, and even if most of his people follow him but then break their oaths of allegiance to him. For a Prophet's prophethood is everlasting.

Do you not see how Sayyidunā Adam ﷺ was a Prophet in the Garden, and he remained so even after he was expelled from it? He is everlasting because he is not shaken, concerned, or disturbed by whatever affliction or trial befalls him. Such is the Everlasting Station: there is no return therefrom, for it is the quarry of perseverance and fixity.

This primordial knowledge that draws assistance from the supreme intellect (*al-ʿaql al-akbar*) is impregnable and unlimited. It brings the divine norms into manifestation as a proverbial talisman. This talisman, moreover, is none other than the *Alif* that manifests itself through multiple Hidden *Alifs*. For the Essence that brought the Primordial *Alif* into existence decreed so beyond time and space, until God placed it into the sensory realm in the form of the staff in the hand of Moses ﷺ, and it will subsist till the Second Coming of Jesus ﷺ.

If you were to behold this created realm with a piercing insight (*naẓra bāṭinīya*), you would discover that all of it is Light. It is like a brilliant full moon that pours forth the Lord's effusion upon non-existent entities. This is where intellects are at a loss to describe the intimations of the Real (*ramzīyat al-ḥaqq*) at this station. To this effect, when Sayyidunā al-Khiḍr ﷺ saw a bird taking a drop from the ocean with its beak, he told Moses ﷺ: "By God, our knowledge in relation to God's knowledge is like the drop in this bird's beak in relation to the ocean." Indeed, it is a drop from the ocean of knowledge of the Chosen One ﷺ. The authority and power of the delimited intellect must borrow from the primordiality of the supreme intellect so that it can encompass the God-given sciences (*'ulūm ladunīya*) which do not become embodied in things. For they are pre-eternal sciences that cannot be understood in the realm of delimitation.

The blessed Messenger ﷺ alluded to his being granted the all-encompassing intellect when he said: "I was given the all-encompassing words (*ūtītu jawāmi' al-kalim*)."[10] That is, he ﷺ was given all the suprasensory meanings, principles, and divine norms to connect the all-encompassing intellect to the delimited intellect. He ﷺ thus described the pleasure of the inhabitants of Paradise and the punishment of the inhabitants of Hell, giving us as it were a general picture to behold before our very eyes. The all-encompassing intellect therefore yields an imaginal form for the delimited intellect, even though the reality of the matter cannot be perceived by the delimited intellect. To this effect, it is related that 'Abdullāh b. 'Abbās said,

---

10   Muslim, *Ṣaḥīḥ*, 1:211.

"Nothing in paradise resembles what is in this world except by name." Similarly, whatever you witness in your disclosure is the manifestation of a delimited attribute or a form; yet its true reality is something different altogether. For everything that you see, dear disciple, is delimited; unless you return to the intellect of the heart that you acquired from the intellect of your Shaykh, who acquired it from Sayyidunā 'Alī ﷺ, the door to the City of Knowledge, who acquired it from the presence of the Chosen One ﷺ, the possessor of the all-inclusive intellect.

The Prophet ﷺ used to say in his supplications: "Dear God, place in my heart Light, and in my sight Light, and in my hearing Light, and to my right Light, and to my left Light, and above me Light, and beneath me Light, and in front of me Light, and behind me Light, and amplify for me Light."[11] The words "and amplify for me Light" refer to the all-inclusiveness of the intellect that the Chosen one ﷺ wished for. Thus the lordly Shaykh bestows upon you the first gleams of Light from the all-encompassing intellect. He tells you that you must have saintly aspiration, truthfulness, and love in order for this dot to yield fruit within you, and in order for you to come to naught in its Light and to become Light yourself. The Path thus begins when you come to naught in the Light and then become Light, and you have no share in primordial knowledge until you pass through these levels. Many have fallen and slipped, and many have returned whence they came. Felicitous is the one who is

11   Ibid., 1:302-303.

granted firmness by God. So beware of thinking that these presences are smooth and easy, for it is necessary to pass beyond the delimited and sensorial intellect, and to seek assistance from the luminous Muḥammadan Intellect so that you may have a share in the subtle graces of these presences.

2.

The Great Tiding
(*al-Naba' al-'Aẓīm*)

Mudhākara from the Friday
Gathering of 5th Ṣafar 1436/28th November 2014

Bismillāh al-Raḥmān al-Raḥīm

Know, dear loved ones, that the Hidden *Alif* is the gushing spring of the presence of the Prophets. It is the station of everlasting life of the ones who occupy the highest levels of proximity from which there is no return. This is why no Prophet who was chosen, elected, and singled out with prophethood has ever broken his vow with God. For it is at this station that the supreme intellect achieves its perfection. This is where you become like a dot, moving through an orbit from presence to presence; or like one who swims in the bezel of the Messenger's ﷺ ringstone.

Know furthermore, may God have mercy on you, that the word "prophethood," *al-nubūwa*, derives from *naba'*, or tiding, and a tiding is a report (*khabar*). The presence of prophethood derives from this tremendous station, the station of the Tremendous Qur'ān (*al-Qur'ān al-Azīm*): **About what do they question one another? About the tremendous tiding (Q**

Naba' 78:1-2). For prophethood is a report that is conveyed on behalf of God. It is a gratuitous favor from God that cannot be acquired, and no one should imagine that it can be earned by way of acquisition. Rather, it is just as God describes it: **I have fashioned thee for Myself.**[12] Acquisition and exertion are for the followers of the Prophets ﷺ, in the form of walking in their footsteps until one inherits their knowledge. "For the scholars are the heirs of the Prophets."[13] So exert yourself in order to attain direct knowledge of this station at the presence of the Hidden *Alif.*

Moreover, given that prophethood is what we call in our Path "the disclosure-site of the supreme intellect and the all-embracing effusion" (*majlā al-'aql al-akbar wa'l-fayḍ al-shāmil*), it is a station that is beyond the intellect and the reflective thoughts that it generates.

Now reflective thought (*fikr*) that is devoid of the remembrance of God (*dhikr*) is a transgression. For reflective thought does not occur except after long periods of remembrance, until your every moment becomes remembrance. To this effect, God says: **Those who remember God standing, sitting, and lying on their sides,**[14] whereupon one becomes worthy of entering into the arena of reflection. For one's inner being is then illuminated by the remembrance of God. This is why God says after praising those who remember Him in every state:

12   Q Ṭāhā 20:41.
13   Abū Dāwūd, *Sunan*, 2:620.
14   Q Āl 'Imrān 3:191.

And they reflect on the creation of the heavens and the earth, 'Our Lord, Thou hast not created this in vain. Glory be unto Thee!'[15] Only then does one profess God's utter transcendence in the manner of the *Kāf* of Immanence (*kāf al-tash-bīh*), proclaiming **glory be to Thee** at each of the twenty levels of the attributes. Thereupon one proclaims the verse: **So shield us from the punishment of the Fire,**[16] because direct knowledge of God must necessarily inspire fear. To this effect, the Prophet ﷺ said, "Of all of you, I know God the best and fear Him the most."[17] Thereafter God [quotes His rememberers as saying]: **Our Lord, whomsoever Thou makest to enter into the Fire, Thou have surely disgraced him; and the wrong-doers shall have no helpers.**[18] The verse comes back to lordship in order for you to know your servanthood toward Him. At that point, the disciple starts to hear what common people do not hear, and to see what others do not see. To this effect, a poet once said:

The hearts of the gnostics possess eyes,
That see what the seers do not see.

As such, a disciple perceives the hidden realities and pure meanings that are bestowed by God upon those whom He

15   Q Āl ʿImrān 3:191.
16   Q Āl ʿImrān 3:191.
17   Zurqānī, *Mukhtaṣar al-maqāṣid*, 165.
18   Q Āl ʿImrān 3:192.

loves. He endows the disciple with a piercing vision (*baṣar ḥadīdī*), a spiritual power, and a subtle grace that lifts the veils of the hidden sciences of proximity. We should note, moreover, that when we say "a spiritual person" (*rūḥānī*) we mean someone who possesses a luminous power, or an inner vision that can return things back to their root. We do not mean *rūḥānī* in the sense of someone who is involved with jinn. For this subtlety of spirit can lift the veils of the sciences of proximity through God's eternal Light. Therefore, genuine pious roaming (*al-siyyāḥa al-ḥaqīqīya*) is to see with the Light of the Real, and to hear with the Light of the Real. It is the Light of the heavens and the earth. It makes itself known to you by assuming likeness (*tamthīl*); **the likeness of His Light** (*mathal nūrih*).[19] This continues until the levels of the Niche, the Lamp, the Resplendent Planet, and the Blessed Tree manifest themselves to you, and the cosmos in its entirety then belongs to you.

You should know, moreover, that God divides and clarifies the souls in the aforementioned Surah 78 entitled al-Naba'. This is why the Surah has come down to us in forty verses, as per the number of souls that are epitomized by God's folk in seven levels. The Surah thus begins with the letters *'Ayn* and

19 **God is the Light of the heavens and the earth; the likeness of His Light is as a niche wherein is a lamp, the lamp in a glass, the glass as it were a glittering star kindled from a Blessed Tree, an olive that is neither of the East nor of the West whose oil well nigh would shine, even if no fire touched it; Light upon Light; God guides to His Light whom He will. And God strikes similitudes for men, and God has knowledge of everything. Q Nūr 24:35.**

Mīm: *'Amma*. The *'Ayn* has seventy levels, as per the seventy veils, whereas the *Mīm* counts as forty levels, which alludes to the perfected Muḥammadan Soul. This is why God says in the Holy Book: **A Messenger has indeed come unto you from your souls.**[20] The seventy marks of faith are thus unveiled, for "faith is divided into seventy-something branches, the lowest of which is to clear harm from the Path."[21] So clear your lower self from the Path, for it is a harm.

As for the verse: **About what do they question one another? About the great tiding regarding which they differ. Nay, but they will know!**[22] Herein is an explicit clarification that when the Lights and spiritual allusions of the Path become manifest and clear, and when they yield hidden, exalted, and luminous secrets, then the souls must necessarily speak about them, and they must differ (*ikhtilāf*) over them. For an heir has a share in the one he inherits from. And just as the Prophets were censured and accused of falsehood, so the saint is tested by being rejected and accused of falsehood. This is especially so when people hear his disciples speak about the Lights and inner secrets that God blessed them with. Some will believe and others will say that these Lights and secrets come from Iblīs. In saying this, it is as if—God forbid!—they were inadvertently saying that darkness comes from God. But the one who ponders the words of God and the words of His Messenger ﷺ will

---

20   Q Tawbah 9:128.
21   Muslim, *Ṣaḥīḥ*, 35.
22   Q Naba' 78:1-5.

find that whenever Light is mentioned, it is ascribed to God or to His Prophet ﷺ. It is also ascribed to the righteous deeds that are prescribed by God's pristine Law. For the true reality of religiosity is to fill the inner realm with divine Lights. Darkness, for its part, is always ascribed to Iblīs, to the false idol (*ṭāghūt*), or to deeds that do not please God and His Messenger ﷺ.

God elucidates the meaning of this battle between the People of Light and the People of Darkness in the following verse: **God is the Friend of those who believe; He brings them out of the darkness into the Light. As for those who disbelieve, their friends are the false idols, bringing them out of the Light into the darkness. They are the inhabitants of the Fire, abiding forever therein.**[23]

This is the Handful of Light that God brought into manifestation within the locus of stillness, so that the realm of non-delimitation became delimited. Prophethood is what occasioned the delimitation of the realm of non-delimitation within the locus of stillness. For the Prophets ﷺ inform us of God, thereby bringing non-delimitation down to the level of delimitation. When people hear about what they convey on behalf of God, some of them believe, and others accuse them of falsehood. What the Prophets ﷺ relate is either a proof for you, the mark of which is that you follow them; or it is a proof against you, the mark of which is that you turn away. God says: **And there will appear unto them from God that which they had not reckoned.**[24]

23   Q Baqara 2:257.
24   Q Zumar 39:47.

You should also know that the revealed Laws were sent down in the measure of the questioning (*al-su'āl*), and some questioning brings with it ease, while other questioning brings with it strictness. This is why the Messenger ﷺ detested questioning that brought no benefit. Hence the prophetic directive that was narrated by Abū Hurayra ؓ: "The Messenger of God ﷺ addressed us and said, 'O people! God has made the Ḥajj obligatory upon you, so perform Ḥajj!' Thereupon a man said: '[Is it to be performed] every year, O Messenger of God?' He ﷺ remained silent, and the man repeated [the question] three times, whereupon the Messenger of God ﷺ said: 'If I were to say 'yes' then it would become obligatory and you would be unable to do it.' Then he ﷺ said: 'Leave me with what I have left to you, for those who came before you were destroyed precisely for excessive questioning, and for opposing their Prophets. When I command you to do anything, do it to the extent of your ability; and when I forbid you from doing something, leave it.'"[25]

The Qur'ān also describes the state of those who were excessive in their questioning. They thereby become strict and cause God to become strict with them. This was the case for the Children of Israel in the story of the cow, and the same holds for the disciple with his Shaykh. The disciple must not question or ask about things that he is unable to commit to. For if he asks and is granted his request, then he is held responsible for what he was granted, and that may ruin him. However, if he is granted

25 Muslim, *Ṣaḥīḥ*, 1:547-548.

something without asking for it, then he must bear patiently and restrain himself because he receives it from God, not from himself.

You should know, dear wayfarer, that you will not be admitted to the Muḥammadan School until your soul becomes purified by the bestowal of the All-Merciful. For **it is God Who purifies whomsoever He wills.**[26] Nonetheless, God has made it obligatory upon you to struggle against your lower self in order to acquire that luminous purity, whereupon the hidden knowledge that was once curtained from you becomes manifest. You should know, moreover, that this knowledge remains hidden from the one who has not arrived at it. Its initial manifestation, with respect to the one who turns his attention to God, is what we call "the beginning." This manifestation begins for each disciple when the Light begins to manifest itself. Each disciple thus has a beginning and an end. At the beginning, you see the light—which you had no previous knowledge of—as a shining star within the heaven of your heart. You then travel upon God's Path until that star, which was your starting point, becomes your endpoint, whereupon you complete the circle of your station.

Since this starting point has multiple properties, each individual looks at it with a different gaze. Yet it remains one in itself, just as the divine names are surrounded by many properties, but their reality remains one. That is why affirming exist-

---

26 Q Nisāʾ 4:49.

ence is intrinsic to the starting point, because the existence of the starting point is attached to the existence of the Real.

You should know, moreover, that every disclosure (*tajallī*) that takes place in existence, whether in the unseen realm or in the visible realm, comes from His name the Manifest (*al-Ẓāhir*). As for the name the Non-Manifest (*al-Bāṭin*), one cannot say that the Real disclosed Himself through His name the Non-Manifest. For a disclosure is a manifestation for the one who experiences the disclosure. The non-manifest therefore remains forever non-manifest, and what discloses itself to you is manifest with respect to you, and non-manifest with respect to others.

3.

The Perfected Soul and the Partial Souls (*al-Nafs al-kāmila wa'l-nufūs al-juz'īya*)

Mudhākara from the Friday
Gathering of 12th Ṣafar 1436/5th December 2014

Bismillāh al-Raḥmān al-Raḥīm

Know, dear wayfarer, that God has placed three main faculties in the human being: the sensory faculty (*al-ḥiss*), the imaginal faculty (*al-khayāl*), and the intellect (*al-ʿaql*). He made each of these three faculties correspond to one of the three worlds: the sensory world (*al-mulk*), the spiritual world (*al-malakūt*), and the world of invincibility (*al-jabarūt*). The human being thus exercises control within each world through its corresponding faculty. Each human being, moreover, inhabits the world that dominates his heart: he is either sensorial, spiritual, or invincible.

As such, the sensorial human being is the one whose heart is stamped by the forms of the sense-objects. He is marked by a dominant love for the herebelow. The spiritual human being is the one whose inward vision (*baṣīra*) has opened up so that he perceives what lies beyond the sensorial realm. Among this type are those who pertain to the lower reaches of the spiritual realm (*al-malakūt al-suflī*), such that the lower spirits among the jinn, the Servants (*khuddām*) and other beings that inhabit this realm become unveiled for them. Others pertain to the higher reaches of the spiritual realm (*al-malakūt al-ʿulwī*), such that the higher spirits among the angels and the saints become unveiled for them. The invincibles (*jabarūtī*), for their part, are those who come to naught and dissolve in God's lordly command (*amrīyat al-rubūbīya*).

At our present age, the human being is dominated by the sensorial world and is overwhelmed by its distractions. He no longer has any knowledge of the spiritual realm nor the realm of invincibility. This is the state that dominates, save those upon whom the Lord has mercy. Felicitous is the one in whom these three faculties are in a state of equilibrium. He is a liminal reality between the three worlds, and none of them veils him from the other. The true knower of God is the one who witnesses the realm of separation (*farq*) within union (*jamʿ*).

As for a Prophet in the presence of gnosis (*ḥadrat al-maʿrifa*), he is in the close company of those brought near (*muqarrabūn*) and is numbered among them. However, his own mountain of selfness is crushed and, as a result, he surpasses the people of nearness who were blessed with illumination by God. He ﷺ referred to this in the tradition, "There is a time for me with God which can contain neither an angel brought near nor a sent messenger." This is a sanctified presence (*ḥadra qud-*

dūsīya). One should not imagine when the Real manifests himself through the commanding soul (*rūḥ amrīya*) that one has reached ultimate nearness and the utmost point of ascension. For there is another sanctified presence above this, a presence whose occupant receives unveiled knowledge about different states, both from the past and the future. Through the power of the senses, he can overpower everything else, and thus he can influence matter. Messengers are given by God the power of the overarching intellect in a sanctified presence, and thus everything obeys their command. They have the right to exercise power over natural things, and everything is subordinate to them in the way that the lower is inherently subordinate to the higher.

The Almighty Real has placed in the Path of wayfarers the means to attain knowledge of Him. The more a disciple's self increases in its detachment, the more it increases in strength. This is because detachment from sensory faculties leads to attachment to the intellect, so that it detaches itself completely from its sensory faculties. The seeker then submits to the intellect, and discovers that its range is broadening around him. As it broadens, the seeker begins to influence his surroundings; and the further the broadening, the greater the influence. This is a prophetic inheritance, a mercy that permeates this nation by virtue of the blessing of our master Muḥammad ﷺ. This is because God has instilled an intellectual power in the Prophet as if he is an angel, and a psychic power through which he knows the movements of the celestial bodies, and likewise a spiritual power. This is why one sees him ruling over people and influencing each world with what suits it.

Know that prophecy is a manifestation of the Almighty Real by way of it being a constitution from our Lord, so that people may know that which they were heedless of, and so that the Laws of [divine] commands, of what is permitted and forbidden, may be apparent to them. Prophecy is thus absolute divine vicegerency (*khilāfa*). The non-restricted divine form is restricted in the form of the prophets, so that every prophet calls on people to God. This is why he ﷺ said, "The saints of God are those who, whenever they are seen, God is remembered."[27] The most perfect, sublime, and noblest of the saints are the Prophets, upon them be blessings and peace. Understand what this means, and beware of restricting yourself to literal constructs.

Know also that the Supreme Spirit (*al-rūḥ al-aʿẓam*) is restricted in this perfected soul. It is because of this that it descends, and then partial souls (*nufūs juzʾīya*) take it on. This is why he ﷺ came and acted, decided, and said what he did, in order to inform them, i.e. the partial souls, about the incomparable divine Essence, by means of an intelligible language. Thus he spoke about these divine names and attributes. Every Prophet from Adam ﷇ to Sayyidunā Muḥammad ﷺ is one of the manifestations of the Supreme Spirit, which is the soul of the Chosen One ﷺ. God says, **There there has come to you a**

---

27 Abū Nuʿaym, *Ḥilya*, 7:271.

Messenger from your souls (*min anfusikum*),[28] meaning from all the souls; therefore His reality is the reality of the Supreme Spirit. Every Prophet is a manifestation of some aspects of this Soul, not its totality. For example, our Master Jesus ﷺ used to bring the dead to life and heal the blind and the leper by the will of God, who manifested Himself unto him through His name the Omnipotent (*al-Qadīr*). He says, **When God said, 'Jesus Son of Mary, remember My blessing upon you and upon your mother, when I confirmed you with the Holy Spirit, to speak to men in the cradle, and of age; and when I taught you the Book, the Wisdom, the Torah, the Gospel; and when you created out of clay, by My leave, as the likeness of a bird, and you blew into it, and it is a bird, by My leave; and you heal the blind and the leper by My leave.**[29] This is so that you may know that every Prophet had a special manifestation of one of the names which appeared prominently through divine omnipotence in the form of miracles, until the Muḥammadan appearance came, whereupon the totality of the names manifested themselves in the Chosen one ﷺ, and thus the beauty of the essence of the intellect was sealed by him. Therefore the Messenger ﷺ preceded all the Prophets in spirit, and was the last among them in form. The last combines what was scattered in those before him.

I would like to note something important here. Seekers learn to close their eyes during their invocation. They have to per-

28   Q Tawba 9:128
29   Q Māʾida 5:112.

form the night vigil (*qiyām al-layl*) prayer to discipline and purify their receptacles, so that they fill with Lights and the locus is cleaned to accommodate God's self-disclosure. There are non-Muslim denominations who perform similar practices that are not compliant with the Islamic Law, disengaging from [worldly] distractions until things whose source they cannot identify start to appear. They believe these to be one thing, while in fact they are something else. It would have been better for them to remain with their distractions than to fill their receptacles with what they do not know. This is why if you were to ask one of them, 'From where did you get this?', they would reply, 'From my own self.' They may worship that which appeared to them, believing it to be a deity, thereby only increasing their misguidance. As for Sufis who perform invocation and follow the Sunnah of the best of creation ﷺ, they invoke the All-Merciful until He discloses Himself to them through His transcendent attributes. They do not believe, however, that what they see is a deity that they must worship. This is because they know God in the way He wishes to be known and in a way that conforms to what the messengers taught. They are therefore immersed in the luminosity of the Real, as described in the verse: **God is the Light of the heavens and the earth.**[30] Such a person is in eternal prostration to the One **who has no like.**[31] This is why we always say, 'meditation without invocation is a violation' (*al-fikr bidūn dhikr ta'addī*). The Most High

30   Q Nūr 24:35.
31   Q Shūrā 42:11.

says, **Those who remember God, standing and sitting and on their sides, and reflect upon the creation of the heavens and the earth.**[32]

Invokers must thus detach themselves from every desire and intention except that which is for God's sake and His pleasure. Everyone performing invocation for the sake of attaining a spiritual station or a secret is mistaken, and their invocation is defective. They must let God direct them, placing them wherever He wills. The disciples must invoke and remember God for the sake of God, until sanctified and luminous manifestations and gifts descend onto their hearts, taking them away from themselves to God.

The launch must be from the Real and the return must be to the Real. As for the ones who begin their spiritual Path in search of their self-interest, they launch from their own selves, and will return to themselves depending on themselves, not their Lord. The ultimate objective of spiritual wayfaring is to reach God. The primary condition is disengagement from all the imaginary forms. Therefore, as a condition for your entering upon the Hidden *Alif* according to the *Hā'*-reading, you must leave your intellect and self behind, rid yourself of all distractions, and enter with a pure spirituality so that you may receive transcendent inrushes from the sanctified presence (*ḥaḍrat al-quds*).

Whoever thinks that just by reading the words of the gnostics in their poems, treatises, and books, they can be like them,

---

32   Q Āl 'Imrān 3:191.

is mistaken. True knowledge is not acquired in this fashion. Rather, it is an illumination (*fatḥ*), an opening from the Real to the heart of a servant who approaches Him with sincerity, disengaging from every obstacle. The words of gnostics are not the very entity of their illumination. Their illumination consists of meanings and experiences that are indescribable. They may express the meaning through description, but the one who is content with the description will lose out on the thing that is described. Understand this.

The point of the words of the gnostics is to inspire people's aspirations so that they may come to know their Creator. A prudent individual must have a special state and time with God, in which he speaks to Him intimately in the last third of the night so that he may expose himself to His holy breezes, and attain transcendental knowledge of Him that is not acquired through the self nor the intellect, until he is awakened from his slumber, as the traditional saying goes, "People are asleep, and when they die, they are awakened." So die voluntarily by passing away in the luminosity of the Real, until those who never really were are annihilated, and He Who always was remains.

4.

The Father of Spirits

Mudhākara from the Friday
Gathering of 19th Ṣafar 1436/12th December 2014

Bismillāh al-Raḥmān al-Raḥīm

Know, may God illuminate your heart through the Light of the Beloved ﷺ, that the Prophets and the saints who inherit their spiritual states live in accordance with the Muḥammadan Reality with respect to bodily form and human traces. For all the Prophets are forms of that true Muḥammadan Reality, including our own Prophet, and those who come after him ﷺ. The Prophets, thus, have become the archetypal realities for the saints among his *Ummah*, and through them all of the worlds have a share in the Muḥammadan Reality.

The knowers of God, moreover, affirm that their sciences, in the furthest extent of their perfection, are nothing but a brand from the spiritual holy Light of this Reality. They only surpass each other in excellence in measure of the differences of Lights among themselves. And it is on account of this Muḥammadan Reality that the Prophets are both the intermediary between the Real and creation, and the reference point in the chain of vertical ascent (*irtiqā' ṣuʿūdī*). The Prophets are thus the possessors of the highest level in this descent of perfection in all of their affairs—their eating, drinking, and clothing, and how they patiently bore abuse from people, to the point that the Master of Creation ﷺ (*sayyid al-khalq*), used to suffer from intense hunger and would place rocks upon his noble stomach. His uncle and his clan waged war against him. He was thrown out of Mecca, the most beloved place unto his heart. His ﷺ noble head was injured, and his teeth were broken, and offal was thrown upon his noble pure back as he prostrated to his Lord in prayer. May my father and mother be his ransom! A hadith relates that Sa'd b. Abī Waqqāṣ ؓ said: "The Prophet ﷺ was asked which people are the most intensely tried. He replied, 'The Prophets, then the ones who are most like them, and so on. A man is tried in proportion to his religion. The one whose religion is solid is granted more solidness [in his trial]; and if his religion is delicate, he is given a lighter one. Trials continue to afflict the servant until he walks upon the earth without a sin to his name.'"[33]

The Prophet ﷺ was the gem of the perfected descendants, and the saints of his community have a portion of that perfection in the measure of their share in that inheritance. Do not presume that you will arrive at sainthood without trial and suffering. The Path to the Garden is riddled with displeasures, and the Path to God is riddled with trials. This is in order for it to clear the dross of your lower self and turn it into pure gold that

---

33   Ibn Ḥibbān, *Ṣaḥīḥ*, 7:161.

is not tainted by the witnessing of anything other than God. Now the more the wayfarer ascends, the more his luminosity intensifies, and the reality of faith imprints itself upon the mirror of his heart, a reality whose oil, kernel, and the quarry of its secret is our Master Muḥammad ﷺ. Given this, he ﷺ is the closest of all things to those who have realized the reality of faith, closer to them than their own souls, property, and families. God says, **The Prophet is closer to the believers than they are to themselves, and his wives are their mothers.**[34] A tradition of the Prophet ﷺ states: "There is no believer except that I am the closest of all mankind to him in this world and in the next. If you wish, recite: **The Prophet is closer to the believers than they are to themselves.**"[35] Thus if he ﷺ were not the father of the spirits and the innermost secret of the existence of incorporeal figures, then he would not be closer to the believer than his own self.

It is related that Ubayy b. Ka'b and Ibn 'Abbās read the verse as: "The Prophet is closer to the believer than their selves, and his wives are their mothers and he is a father to them (*wa huwa ab lahum*)." Similar readings were also attributed to Mu'āwiya, Mujāhid, 'Ikrima, and al-Ḥasan.

In a tradition the Prophet ﷺ said "I am just like your father, I teach you. If one of you must defecate, let them not face the *qibla*, nor give their back to it, nor wipe with their right hand."[36]

---

34 Q Aḥzāb 33:6.
35 Bukhārī, *Ṣaḥīḥ*, 2:987.
36 Abū Dāwūd, *Sunan*, 1:3.

Thus this verse from Surat al-Aḥzāb alludes to the spiritual fatherhood that is specific to the believers. That is why the verse happens to be the sixth verse in the Surah, as an allusion to the *wāw* of faith (*wāw al-īmān*) because the value of the *wāw* in the alphabetical numerical system is six. Thereafter, the wayfarer comes to naught in the *Hā'*, whose numerical value is five, through annihilation in the acts by virtue of the five pillars on the level of Islam: the testimony of faith, prayer, fasting, almsgiving, and the pilgrimage. Then after realizing the first principle (*al-aṣl al-awwal*) he enters into the reality of faith and direct tasting of its innermost secrets through the six levels of faith: faith in God, His angels, His books, His Messengers, the Last Day, and the good and evil of destiny. At that point, the innermost secret of He (*Huwa*) is unveiled for you by virtue of the *Hā'*-reading of the divine name *Allāh*. Therefore, it is in the measure of your ascension in faith that you come to have direct tasting and witnessing of this prophetic spirit. The believers (*al-mu'minūn*) in the verse, then, are the knowers; for the believer is the one who knows himself, and when you come to know that you are a sinner, a disobedient one with no power or authority, except through God; at that point, you become a knower of God with direct tasting, not in word alone. The Prophet ﷺ is therefore closest to the knowers. This is why his wives are their mothers, taking into account the aspect of this reality that is embodied by the Muḥammad Light, which the Real manifested to some and not to others. This is why the wives of the Prophet ﷺ are our mothers, because he ﷺ is our spiritual father. It is an exalted and sublime fatherhood, for were the Prophet ﷺ in his own luminous reality not the cause of all existents, then he would not be closer to you than your own self, and closer to you than all that you own.

As for the verse, **Muḥammad is not the father of any man among you,**[37] this is not intended to deny the spiritual fatherhood nor to deny the biological fatherhood that he has towards his children whom God took back before they attained the age of maturity. Nor does it deny his fatherhood toward his daughters—may God's good pleasure be upon all of them. Rather, this noble verse addresses his marriage to Zaynab after she had been divorced by Zayd b. Ḥāritha, whom the Prophet ﷺ had adopted before the prohibition of adoption. Thus God revealed these noble verses in order to dispel what had arisen in the hearts of some people who looked unfavorably on the marriage of the Prophet ﷺ to the ex-wife of the man he had previously adopted. Thus God declared that adoption was no longer valid, nor governed by the rulings that govern true fatherhood. Thus He said: **And remember thou said unto him whom God has blessed and whom thou has blessed, "Retain your wife for yourself in reverence to God." Thou wast hiding in thyself that which God was to disclose, and thou didst fear the people, though God has more right to be feared by thee. Then when Zayd relinquished his claim upon her, we wed her to thee so that there should be no restriction for the believers in**

37   Q Aḥzāb 33:40.

respect to the wives of their adopted sons when the latter have relinquished their claims upon them. And the command of God shall be fulfilled; there is no restriction for the Prophet in what God has ordained for him. That is the wont of God with those who passed away before, and God's command is a decree determined. Those who convey God's messages and fear Him and fear none but God and God suffices as a reckoner. Muḥammad is not the father of any man among you; rather, he is the Messenger of God and the Seal of Prophets; and God is Knower of all things.[38]

This verse, by way of allusion, speaks of the soul with its forty levels of perfection. This is why the number of the verse in the Surat al-Aḥzāb is forty. Thus the reality of this level is that drawing from the Chosen One ﷺ, and taking directly from him, is greater than taking from Gabriel عليه السلام. Which is to say that there is nothing higher than the God's Messenger ﷺ. Thus Gabriel, the Archangel, is a vizier of prophethood. And this lower dot (*nuqṭa*) of the *Bā'* entails subjugating one's self in a state of abasement and servanthood vis-à-vis the exaltedness of Lordship. And you might say that Gabriel عليه السلام is the supreme spirit (*al-rūḥ al-aʿẓam*), or we can say that he is the first expansion, by which all creatures subsist. As prophethood stands out by the distinct characteristic of expansion as well as vicegerency, he is the principle of existentiation (*al-aṣl al-takwīnī*).

---

38   Q Aḥzāb 33:37-40.

For the Prophet's ﷺ prophethood is a prophethood of existentiation. It is not simply prophethood that is restricted to guidance and instruction.

Prophethood in this sense has many manifestation-sites, and its greatest one is Sayyidunā Muḥammad ﷺ, in terms of his bodily form. And in the hadith he says, "I was the first among the prophets in creation and the last of them in being sent forth."[39] And in another hadith: "When God created Adam عليه السلام, he told him of his offspring, and he began to look at the prophets, upon them be peace, and the virtues of some of them over others. He noticed a shining Light beneath them and said, 'My Lord, who is that?' He said, 'That is your son Aḥmad; he is the first and the last, and he is the first intercessor.'"[40] He ﷺ is therefore first among the prophets, and he is the last prophet. It is as if he ﷺ is telling you that he is the luminous handful as explained in the tradition of Jābir.[41]

39   Translator's note: This report is sometimes cited in tafsīr literature (e.g. Ṭabarī's commentary on Q Aḥzāb 33:7 in *Jāmiʿ al-bayyān ʿan taʾwīl āy al-Qurʾān*). Its meaning is corroborated by other hadiths, including the following: "The Prophet was asked: 'When did prophethood become incumbent upon you?' He replied: 'When Adam was still between spirit and body.'" Tirmidhī, *Sunan*, 2:924.

40   Ṣāliḥī, *Subul al-rashād*, 1:91.

41   Translator's note: The tradition in question is related by Jābir b. ʿAbd Allāh who asked the Prophet: "O Messenger of God, may my father and mother be your ransom, tell me of the first thing God created? He said: 'O Jābir, the first that God created was the Light of your prophet...'" This hadith occupies an important place in Sufi writings, although it does not meet the standards of most Sunni hadith transmitters. The modern hadith scholar Albānī, for instance, considers it to be a false report (*bāṭil*) (*Silsilat al-aḥādīth*, 1:820). Nonetheless, the doctrine the

You should also know that with respect to the Hidden *Alif*, when we speak of the station of prophethood, we are not speaking with respect to the forms of the prophets. Rather, we are speaking with respect to this prophethood of existentiation, which is not delimited by a form. For the inner dimension of prophethood is the sainthood of the Prophet 鄉, and that is the Luminous Handful (*al-qabḍa al-nūrānīya*). This is why the station of gnosis (*maʿrifa*) entails the Prophet's precedence in view of the fact that he is the Perfect Man in his time. This is because he possesses the prophethood of existentiation, which is the delegating authority that speaks for and of God—**And when your Lord said to the Angels, "I am placing a vicegerent upon the earth"**[42]—and the first intellect, which encompasses all things in knowledge. His inheritors among the righteous also have a share in this prophetic inheritance. God says, **God is the Light of the heavens and the earth,**[43] which is to say that creation subsists through the secret of His name the Sustaining (*al-Qayyūm*) by virtue of the Luminous Handful, in which all knowledge is enfolded, as well as all that was and all that will be. This is why the Prophet 鄉 is the intermediary between the Real and creation both outwardly and inwardly.

Muḥammadan Light (*al-nūr al-muḥammadī*) has been upheld by Sufis on the basis of many scriptural and theological grounds, including more rigorously authenticated hadiths such as the Prophet's statement: "I was a Prophet while Adam was between spirit and body." (Tirmidhī, *Sunan*, 3609).

42   Q Baqara 2:30.

43   Q Nūr 24:35.

5.

God Created him in His Image
(*Khalaqahu Allāh ʿalā Ṣūratihi*)

Mudhākara from the Friday
Gathering of 26th Ṣafar 1436/19th December 2014

Bismillāh al-Raḥmān al-Raḥīm

Know, may God adorn your inner vision with the *kohl* of the niche of prophethood, that the presence of prophethood is the disclosure-site of inerrancy (*ʿiṣma*), and of the oath of allegiance and everlastingness. When we speak of it, we speak through the gate of sainthood; that is to say, through the sainthood of the Prophet ﷺ. This is by virtue of the descent of the subtle luminous graces from the heart of the Prophet ﷺ upon the heart of the saint, through the initiatic chain that is connected directly back to him. As for the presence of prophethood itself, no one except for the Prophet ﷺ can speak regarding it.

Now it is known by self-evident necessity that every messenger is a prophet and every prophet is a saint. But the inverse is not true, because a prophet or a messenger, before the descent of revelation upon him, was a saint, and his sainthood preceded his prophethood. You should always remember this principle when you read what we say. You should also keep in mind that the speech of the Messenger ﷺ sometimes issues from the circle of his messengerhood, sometimes from the circle of his prophethood, and other times from the circle of his sainthood. Each of these circles has its own Light through which it is identified. None directly tastes the spirit of his words and the niche of his manifestation, except the one whose inner vision has opened, and whose inmost secret has become purified, until it fully discloses itself and becomes a mirror that shows him the entirety of existence.

Given that this is the case, the way to attainment hinges upon following the traces by way of emulation and annihilation in the Lights of the Followed One ﷺ, outwardly and inwardly. This cannot be achieved except by traversing the Path at the hands of a Shaykh who knows the pathways. One who has scooped up marvelous realities from the ocean of Muḥammadan Light, that you may follow the counsel of your Lord, who says: **Follow the way of those who turn in repentance unto Me,**[44] and: **O you who believe, revere God and be with the truthful.**[45]

You should know, moreover, that the Perfect Man (*al-insān al-kāmil*) who was chosen by the Real and granted divine knowledge through direct witnessing (*shuhūd*) and eye-witnessing (*ʿiyān*), and the most fulfilled life, is the Adamic human being of the Garden who was taught by God all of the names: **And He taught Adam all the names.**[46] Thus, he became worthy

44 Q Luqmān 31:15.
45 Q Tawba 9:119.
46 Q Baqara 2:31.

of the vicegerency of the names (*al-khilāfa al-asmā'iya*) and became a liminal reality (*barzakh*) between the Real and creation, with one face turned toward the Exalted presence by virtue of his spirituality, and one face turned toward creation by virtue of his human nature. Upon knowing all the names directly, he became absent in the Named. He is thus the absent present, the annihilated subsisting one. Or you might say that he has one face turned toward Lordship by virtue of the inblowing of the Spirit—**and I blew into him of My Spirit;**[47] **Say: the Spirit is from the command of my Lord**[48]—and another face turned toward servanthood by virtue of the handful of clay: **When your Lord said to the Angels, "I am creating a human being from clay."**[49] The Prophet ﷺ said, "God created Adam from a handful that he collected from all of the earth, and the children of Adam came forth in proportion to the earth. Among them are the red, the white, the black, and those in between. Among them are those who are fortunate, sad, lowly, goodly, and those in between."[50]

The Perfect Man is thus the one who brings together the realities from the two presences of the Real and creation. He thus possesses two forms: an outward one and an inward one. With respect to his outward form, we find that he possesses everything that is in creation, because he brings together the

47   Q Ḥijr 15:29.
48   Q Isrā' 17:85.
49   Q Ṣād 38:71.
50   Abū Dāwūd, *Sunan*, 2:788.

four natural elements (*al-ṭabāʾiʿ al-arbaʿa*) from which the Real created all things, which are earth, air, fire and water. These four elements encompass all created things, and the human being brings all this together, as alluded to in a verse ascribed to Sayyidunā ʿAlī :

> *You believe yourself to be a small body,*
> *But within you is enfolded the greater world.*

And as far as his inner form is concerned, he is the one who has attained the honor of being created in the form of the Real, as alluded to in the prophetic tradition, "God created Adam in His form,"[51] and in another, "The child of Adam was created in the form of the All-Merciful."[52]

Note how he cited the all-encompassing name *Allāh* and its vizier, the name the All-Merciful (*al-Raḥmān*), as an allusion to the all-inclusive totality upon which the inner form of the complete human being is created. This is because these two names are not surpassed in elevation or in rank except by the Supreme Hidden Name (*al-ism al-aʿẓam al-maknūn*). This is why the human being is the supreme creation in the full sense of the term. He is the only created entity that is worthy of vicegerency of the names, since it is none other than the reality of his inner true form, upon which he was created as per the hadith. Thus it is the secret of the All-Hearing that he hears, and by the Light

51 Bukhārī, *Ṣaḥīḥ*, 3:1267-1268.
52 ʿAsqalānī, *Fatḥ al-Bārī*, 5:217.

of the All-Seeing that he sees, and by the secret of the Speaking that he speaks, and by the secret of the Willing that he wills, and by the secret of the All-Powerful that he has power, and so on. The Perfect Man being is the site of total manifestation that brings together all the names.

Moreover, when we say the outward form, we do not just mean the body. Rather, we mean the body, the soul, the heart, the intellect, and the spirit (*al-jasad, al-nafs, al-qalb, al-ʿaql, al-rūḥ*). The spirit, the intellect, and others are but stations through which the wayfarer passes, because this is the Path that leads to the Real. The proof that the spirit falls under the realm of the outward is the fact that you see Light, because it is an outward vision. However, the one who has arrived at direct vision of the Command's Spirit stands at the threshold of the door of the inner secrets of the world of invincibility. This is because the inner dimension is knowledge of the innermost secrets of the names, through which you come to perceive the inner meaning of the true form upon which Adam was created, without any suggestion of indwelling or unification or intermingling. The outward form of the Perfect Man includes bodily density in the physical world of dominion, as well subtlety of spirit in the spiritual realm. As for the inner form, it is the innermost secrets of the realm of invincibility.

Or from a different perspective, we could say that the spirit is from the command of lordship (*al-rūḥ min amr al-rubūbīya*). It is one of the self-disclosures of the name the Lord, which bequeaths the disclosures in the realm of separation. This is why it falls under the outward form of the Perfect Man. As for the inner form, it is a form of union, not a form of separation, which is why the prophetic tradition cites the all-encompassing name *Allāh*, and why God commanded His angels to prostrate to Adam, and they prostrated to that inner form.

You should know, furthermore, that the Perfect Man is the spirit of the cosmos. He possesses primordiality and finality. Thus, he is the first with respect to the Luminous Handful (*al-qabḍa al-nūrāniya*). God's Messenger ﷺ said, "When God created Adam ﷺ, he told him of his offspring, and he began to look at the Prophets, upon them be peace, and the virtues of some of them over others. He noticed a shining Light beneath them and said, 'My Lord, who is that?' He said, 'That is your son Aḥmad; he is the first and the last, and he is the first intercessor.'"[53] Thus, the status of primordiality is linked to the station of his prophethood ﷺ, which is why he ﷺ said, "I was a Prophet while Adam was between spirit and body."[54] Then he ﷺ is the last with respect to his created nature and his cosmic spatial form, that he may seal prophethood through his station of finality (*ākhirīya*), just as he opened it with his status of primordiality (*awwalīya*). The circle returns to the dot whence it began, the ringstone of the seal comes to manifest.

You should know furthermore, dear wayfarer, that the one who enters the most-holy presence (*al-ḥadra al-aqdasīya*) goes missing (*mafqūd*), because the one whom God permits to enter

---

53   Ṣāliḥī, *Subul al-rashād*, 1:91.
54   Ibn Abī Shaybah, *Muṣannaf*, 13:204-205.

it will not find therein himself, let alone any other. As for the presence of the divan (*ḥaḍrat al-dīwān*), you find therein the saints and the Poles (*aqṭāb*, sing. *quṭb*). The latter is an outward presence, not an inward presence. You should also know that the Perfect Man is small by way of his corporeal entity, and subtle in form, rapid in movement. When he moves, all of the cosmos moves with him. This is why in his retreats (*khalwa*) when he invokes the Name *Allāh*, he moves the planets, the stars, the sun, and the moon. This indicates that when he looks at the cosmos at that point, he beholds its true form, the form that God created it upon. When he calls out, the divine names turn towards him. It is for this reason that the Perfect Man is the spirit of the cosmos, and the cosmos has no power to subsist without him. It is to him that the tradition of the Prophet ﷺ alludes when he said, "The Hour will not come to pass until 'Allāh, Allāh' is no longer uttered upon the earth."[55] Thus, the Perfect Man is the last to ascend and the first to descend. This is why the Beloved ﷺ encompassed this perfection through both the primordiality of prophethood by virtue of the primacy of the spirit; as well as the finality of prophethood by virtue of the sensorial manifestation of his noble presence ﷺ. Thus, he brought it together in a complete and total manner through his primacy.

Dear wayfarer, the everlasting presence (*ḥaḍrat al-khūlud*) is the first principle and the last one, because it lifts the veil

---

55   Muslim, *Ṣaḥīḥ*, 1:74.

from the meaning of the Perfect Man. Whoever knows him knows everything, and whoever does not know him is ignorant of everything. It was to this meaning that the Shaykh of our Shaykhs Sayyidī Aḥmad al-'Alawī, may God be pleased with him, referred in one of his poems when he spoke on behalf of the Muḥammadan Reality and said, "O you who desires to perceive my craft (*yā man turīd tadrī fannī*)" as well as other poems which revolve around this meaning. For the Muḥammadan Reality is the kernel of the Perfect Man. Thus, the vicegerency of the knowers of God is specific to the Perfect Man, because the vicegerent must resemble the form of the one whose vicegerent he is. The saint is the one who was brought out from the darkness into the Light, as God says, **God is the Friend of those who believe, He brings them out from the darknesses into the Light.**[56] As for the vicegerent, he is the one whom God has appointed in His stead in order to bring mankind out from the darkness into the Light. He is thus the true servant of God, and the cosmos and all that it contains are subordinate to him. In fact, were it not for him, none of it would have become manifest at all. Ibn 'Abbās ﷺ said, "One of the things that God revealed to Jesus ﷺ was, 'Believe in Muḥammad ﷺ, and command those of your community who are his contemporaries to believe in him too. For were it not for Muḥammad ﷺ, I would not have created Adam. Were it not for Muḥammad, I would not have created the Fire. I created the Throne upon the water, and it

---

56   Q Baqara 2:257.

shook, and then I wrote upon it, *lā ilāha illā Allāh, Muḥammad rasūl Allāh*, and it became still.'"[57]

You should know furthermore, that the Prophet ﷺ is the supreme spirit (*al-rūḥ al-aʿẓam*) who is expressed by the word *al-Khalīfa*, the vicegerent, whereas prophethood is an expression of the receptivity of the holy soul for the realities that are known of God through an intermediary. This has two states. The first is outward, reacting to the first intellect, however the command may be. The second is the inwardness of sainthood. Thus, it is clear that the Muḥammadan Reality is the ink and the essence of the first intellect. It is a representation of the beginning of creation and its end. It is the first before every before, because the first thing that God brought into manifestation in the chain of created existence was his Light ﷺ; and it is the last in the attribute of the human spatial form. He ﷺ is the most noble creation in the absolute sense, and the supreme loved one whom God brought into manifestation in the presence of the divine actions as a "walking Qurʾān." It is he who possesses prophethood, vicegerency, and sainthood by way of primacy. As for the other prophets, they possessed prophethood through deputyship to his noble presence. They were thus the forms of the Muḥammadan Reality before the manifestation of the ringstone of the seal. Likewise, his heirs among the saints of his nation are the forms of the Muḥammadan Reality within the circle of sainthood following his ﷺ noble manifestation. This is

57   Ḥakim, *Mustadrak*, 2:722.

why a disciple must exert effort in order to see Light before all things, for all of creation was created from his ﷺ Light.

You should also know that the worthiest creatures of the station of sainthood, after the prophets and the noble companions, may God be pleased with them, are the People of the Household of the Prophet ﷺ, because they are closest to the first principle. They are most worthy of the intermediacy of the intermediary of existentiation, because every existent thing possesses existence through their love, and those deprived of their love do not exist in the first place, because their love is a beautiful deed (*ḥasana*), and a beautiful deed is Light. It is related that Ibn ʿAbbās said of God's words, **And whosoever accomplishes a beautiful deed,** "Love for the Prophet and his household is that beautiful deed."[58] Thus, the love of creation is a ray from their Light, and those who are goodly are from their configuration, and they are the ones who are closest to the Light. As for others, they are closest to the ray, not to the Light itself. As for those who are not goodly, it is from the reflection of their darkness, because their hatred is an ugly deed, and an ugly deed is a darkness in the heart. That is why the Messenger ﷺ said, "Love God for all the blessings that He imparts upon you, and love me on account of your love for God, and love the people of my house on account of your love for me."[59] Thus, the sequential chain of love comes to manifest. Our love for the Prophet's

---

58　Mentioned by Suyūṭī in *Iḥyā faḍāʾil Ahl al-Bayt*, based on a narration by Ibn Abī Ḥātim. See Suyūṭī, *Iḥyāʾ faḍāʾil Ahl al-Bayt*, 17.

59　Tirmidhī, *Sunan*, 2:963.

family directs us to the love of their grandfather ﷺ, and loving him ﷺ is part of loving God.

You should know, moreover, that the sainthood of the Prophet ﷺ is wider in scope than his prophethood, and his prophethood is wider in scope than his messengerhood. You could say by way of illustration that an olive has a peel, a kernel, and oil. The message is the husk, prophethood is the kernel, and sainthood is the oil. All of this concerns the essence of the Prophet ﷺ, not others. Likening the messengerhood to the peel is not to belittle its status, far from it. Our intention is to illustrate its manifestation, because the message is intense in its manifestation, just as the peel is manifest over the kernel, and the kernel is manifest over the oil. The oil is more hidden than the kernel because it only manifests after obliteration and effacement. Understand this.

Sainthood, which is a prophetic inheritance, flows through this blessed Muḥammadan nation by virtue of the scholars who are the heirs of the Prophets. It discloses itself in two sorts: a sainthood that is eternal and essential, pertaining to the Real, and this is absolute sainthood (*wilāyat al-iṭlāq*) whose manifestation-site is the Seal; and a sainthood that is derived from absolute sainthood. The former saint is a renewer (*mujaddid*) who establishes foundational principles. The second is a follower of these foundational principles, and does not veer from them, because he has no power to establish new foundational principles of wayfaring through the levels of the Name. Both of them hark back to the Muḥammadan Reality, and both of them are from the People of the Household of the Chosen One ﷺ. Prophethood has been sealed inasmuch as the giving of tidings (*naba'*) is concerned, and it is only sainthood that will forever remain with respect to exercising authority over souls, because the gate of sainthood remains open whereas the gate of prophethood was closed with the sending forth of our Prophet, Sayyidunā Muḥammad ﷺ.

6.

Sanctity is the Gate of Prophethood (*al-Wilāya Bāb al-Nubūwa*)

Mudhākara from the Friday
Gathering of 25th Rabīʿ al-Awwal 1436/16th January 2015

Bismillāh al-Raḥmān al-Raḥīm

You should know, dear wayfarer, that when we speak of the Seal of Sanctity, this means the highest station of Light in the liminal *Alif* between the ocean of prophethood and the ocean of messengerhood. It is a direct inheritance from the possessor of the all-holy effusion ﷺ. As for the Seal of the prophethood of prophets, it has been sealed in the presence of the Chosen One, al-Muṣṭafā ﷺ, because it is through him that the circle of prophethood was closed, and the ringstone of the Muḥammadan Seal came to manifest. This is alluded to in the tradition of the Prophet ﷺ in which he said, "When God created Adam ﷺ, he told him of his offspring, and he began to look at the Prophets, upon them be peace, and the virtues of some of them over others. He noticed a shining Light beneath them and said, 'My Lord, who is that?' He said, 'That is your son Aḥmad; he is the first and the last, and he is the first intercessor.'"[60]

You should also know that it is forbidden for any prophet among the prophets, or any saint beneath them, to enter upon the divine presence after God has sealed prophethood and messengerhood by sending Sayyidunā Muḥammad ﷺ, except through the gate of sainthood. And we say "any prophet among the prophets" because when Jesus ﷺ descends at the end of time, it will be as a follower of Sayyidunā Muḥammad ﷺ. He will not come down with a new revealed Law, because the gate of prophethood was closed by Sayyidunā Muḥammad ﷺ. Thus he will be a complete and perfected Muḥammadan saint. The supreme station of sainthood, in view of the fact that it is a complete manifestation-site for the comprehensiveness of the Supreme Name, belongs to the Seal of prophets Sayyidunā Muḥammad ﷺ. Its inner dimension is his, and its outward dimension is for the saints of his nation. He ﷺ said in a tradition, "The scholars are the heirs of the prophets."[61] Therefore, in respect of its manifestation in the visible realm, and in order for it not to be hidden from anyone, it will belong to the universal Seal of sanctity which is Sayyidunā ʿĪsā ﷺ.

You should also know that this commanding authority (*amrīya*) was appointed by God in the sensory realm as an intermediary between the saints by virtue of sainthood, and between the prophets by virtue of prophethood. For its reality

60   Ṣāliḥī, *Subul al-rashād*, 1:91.
61   Abū Dāwūd, *Sunan*, 2:620.

is one, but it has many different descents of perfection whether by way absoluteness or restrictiveness. For the prophets, upon them be peace, are all perfected, but there is a hierarchy of degrees of excellence among them. The peak of the level of perfection in the absolute sense belongs to Sayyidunā Muḥammad ﷺ, which is why he completely descended into human nature until other creations displayed animosity toward him, and he experienced poverty and various forms of harm.

You should also know that each human being has a glimmer of the Light, as the Prophet ﷺ said, "When God created Adam, He wiped over his back and from it descended all the offspring that He created until the Day of Resurrection, and He placed between the eyes of each human being among them a glimmer of Light. He displayed them before Adam, who said, 'My Lord, who are they?' God said, 'These are your offspring.' [Adam] saw among them a man and he wondered at the glimmer of Light between his eyes, and said, 'My Lord who is that?' God said, 'This is a man from the final communities of your offspring. His name is Dāwūd.' He said, 'My Lord, how long will he live?' He said 'Sixty years.' He said, 'My Lord, give him forty more years from my own lifetime.' And when the lifetime of Adam came to an end, the angel of death came to him, and Adam said, 'Don't I have forty years left?' The angel said, 'Did you not give them to your son Dāwūd?' But he denied, and so did his offspring; and he forgot, and so did his offspring; and he erred, and so did his offspring."[62] This luminous glimmer will bear witness over all mankind on the Day of Resurrection.

Moreover, this tradition has the answer to anyone who doubts in the Light that the wayfarers witness in their hearts. You hear them say things like, "This Light which the people of the Path see has no special characteristics and no importance, because we see and hear that other groups among non-Muslims also see Lights when they engage in spiritual exertion." Yet we say that this Light that anyone else sees may well be that glimmer that was placed by God between the eyes of each human being, because it is within them. Whoever diminishes the trace of the sensory faculties will begin to have an inner vision, and that glimmer will manifest for him. Yet this light has no special distinction insofar as attaining the knowledge of God is concerned. Rather, God placed it among mankind in order to realize His name the Just (*al-ʿAdl*), and as a manifestation-site of the inner disposition upon which He created them.

As for the Light that the people of our Order speak of, it is a pure lordly Light that God casts into the heart of whomever of His servants He wishes. It is the key to ascend into the spiritual realm of the heavens and the earth. It is the Path of disclosure of the names and attributes in the hearts of the wayfarers. It is the Path of annihilation, coming to naught, and dissolving in the Essence. This is why you find that the other sects who see that luminous glimmer are as distant from God as can be. You

---

62   Tirmidhī, *Sunan*, 2:778.

find them devoting themselves to worship of other-than-God. As for the Light that is drawn from God through the intermediacy of the Shaykhs of spiritual training, it is the one that makes you cling more to God's revealed Law, because it takes you in your entirety and casts you into prostration in the presence of God. Then it draws you near to the quarry of Light, Sayyidunā Muḥammad ﷺ, until you see him. Thus, you find that the more the disciple travels upon the Muḥammadan Path, the stronger the Light grows in his heart, the more it flows over his entire being. And the further he strays from the revealed Law and plunges into disobedient acts, the smaller the Light becomes in his heart, until it almost fades and extinguishes entirely. Thus, there is no comparison between the Light that increases in radiance and in intensity when the servant preserves the oil of the revealed Law, and the Light that flickers in the heart of one who does not know God and does not follow His Law.

Moreover, the Light of faith is attained through sincerity of following (*ittibāʿ*). As for the other light, it is attained by following a specific modality that falls outside the gates of the revealed Law. Moreover, the Light that God's folk speak of is alluded to in many verses and noble statements of the Prophet ﷺ, including God's words, **What of the one who is dead and to whom we gave life, and placed with him a Light by which he walks among mankind?**[63] as well as the verse, **O you who believe, reverence God and believe in His Messenger, He will give**

---

63   Q Anʿām 6:122.

you a twofold portion of His mercy and make a Light for you by which you may walk, and forgive you.[64] Note the Qur'ānic mode of expression in these two noble verses, how it uses verbal expressions that leave no room for allegorical interpretation because of its intense clarity. Namely, walking in the Light that is sent down from God into the heart. So be among those who pay regard to this divine expression. God says: **God is the Light of the heavens and the earth; a likeness of His Light is as a niche in which is a lamp, the lamp is in a glass, (and) the glass is as it were a brightly shining star, lit from a blessed olive-tree, neither eastern nor western, the oil whereof almost gives Light though fire touch it not—light upon light! God guides to His Light whom He pleases, and God sets forth parables for men, and God is Cognizant of all things.**[65] It is related that Ubayy b. Ka'b ﷺ said of His words, **the likeness of His Light,** "He spoke of the Light of the believer and said, **the likeness of His Light,** as though He were saying, 'the likeness of the believer's light.'" Ubayy actually used to recite it that way, with "the likeness of the believer." Ibn 'Abbās went to Ka'b al-Aḥbār, God be pleased with him, and said, "Tell me about the verse, **God is the Light of the heavens and the earth.** Ka'b replied, "God is the Light of the heavens and the earth, the likeness of His Light is like Muhammad ﷺ, like a niche." Reflect on how, in this verse, Light is connected to guidance, so that you may come to know how the Light of guidance that is seen inwardly by the wayfar-

64 Q Ḥadīd 57:28.
65 Q Nūr 24:35.

ers is the very essence of God's guidance to His servants.

The Beloved ﷺ said, "God created His creation in darkness, and cast some of His Light upon it. The one whom that Light touched is guided, and the one whom it escaped goes astray. That is why I say that the pen has dried regarding God's knowledge."[66] What was ordained for the servants in pre-eternity must necessarily occur. For the one who was touched by the Light of the Real in pre-eternity, it will manifest for him in space and time; and as for the one who was not touched by the Light in pre-eternity, it will not touch him in the spatial realm. This cast Light is what distinguishes between guidance and misguidance. It is the mark of guidance. As for the luminous glimmer that was placed between the eyes of each human being, it flows through the guided and the errant alike. So let those who doubt the subtle Lights of the Real in the hearts of some of His creatures ask themselves: what is it that they deny? They should fear for themselves as they plunge into that which they have no knowledge. If the only punishment meted out to those who doubt and deny the Light of faith that manifests in the hearts of the disciples were that they were deprived of this Light themselves, it would be a sufficient punishment.

You should know, moreover, that the knower of God ascends in the levels of the intellect and the soul, then in the spiritual realm, and into the realm of invincibility. He experiences this only through the Lights of the Lord, until he becomes annihi-

66 Tirmidhī, *Sunan*, 673.

lated. It is in this regard that we say that the one who is at the station of the Hidden *Alif* should not speak about his body or his corporeality, because the one who remains with his sensory faculties has no share in this station.

You should also know, may God have mercy upon you, that the Qur'ān is the first Pen of the Real, and that all the revealed books correspond to a part of its whole. First there was the Qur'ān, and from it the rest of the revealed books flowed forth. The Lights of the Qur'ān manifest so long as the Muḥammadan life-breaths flow through you. By their means, you receive understandings of the Qur'ān and the gnostic sciences with ease, and you enter into the honor of being associated with God's folk. The Prophet ﷺ said, "God has special people among mankind. They said, 'O Messenger of God, who are they?' He ﷺ said, 'They are the people of the Qur'ān, the people of God and His elect.'"[67] The Qur'ān is thus the all-encompassing tablet which contains the news of those who came before and those who come after. It is the guide and mentor of the wayfarers. It is their proof at every station that they occupy or pass through. So when you recite the Qur'ān by virtue of the Hidden *Alif* you will see it to be disentangled from all cosmic forms.

You should know, moreover, that the three realms, the physical (*mulk*) the spiritual (*malakūt*) and the realm of invincibility (*jabarūt*), interpenetrate with each other. This is why there are multiple forms of receiving revelation and taking it from

---

67   Ibn Mājah, *Sunan*, 78.

the presence everlasting at the station of prophethood of the Chosen One ﷺ. Sometimes he would take it directly from God with no intermediacy; sometimes through the intermediary of the angel of revelation; sometimes he would hear the speech of God in this sensory domain; and sometimes it would be a spiritual gaze (*naẓra malakūtīya*) that manifested in the sensory realm of the world of dominion, such as the manifestation of Gabriel علیه السلام in the form of the Companion Diḥya al-Kalbī.

You should know, moreover, that when you recite the noble Qur'ān, you discover an inner sublime coloring, just as you find there to be a dense coloring of human nature, as per the verse, **Say: I have no power over what benefit or harm may come to me, save as God will. Had I knowledge of the unseen, I would have acquired much good, and no evil would have touched me. I am but a warner and a bearer of glad tidings unto a people who believe,**[68] as well as the verse, **Say: I am no innovation among the messengers, and I know not what will be done with me or with you. I only follow that which was revealed unto me, and I am but a clear warner,**[69] as well as the verse, **Say: I am only a human being like you; it is revealed unto me that your God is one God. So whoever hopes for the meeting with his Lord, let him perform righteous deeds and make no one a partner unto his Lord in worship.**[70] Here, God affirms the Prophet's human nature as well as his special status.

68 Q A'rāf 7:188.
69 Q Aḥqāf 46:9.
70 Q Kahf 18:110.

Why then should we deny the people of the inner coloring? The attribute of human nature does not contradict the manifestation of God's attentive care: "I become the hearing with which he hears, and the seeing with which he sees," in a manner that is hallowed beyond any suggestion of indwelling and unification.

The human nature of the Prophet ﷺ is a unique pearl and precious jewel, to the point that God declares the unbelief of the one who equates the soul of the Prophet with any other soul. God says, **That is because their Messengers brought them clear proofs at which they said, 'Shall a human being guide us?' So they disbelieved and turned away, yet God is unneedy and praised.**[71] He ﷺ came in the human form in order to teach us how to travel the spiritual Path, because God is not analogous to anything, and so His knowledge cannot come to us except by assuming the shape of a human form like ours, that is specially elected by Him. God says, **Thus we have revealed unto thee a spirit from Our command. Thou knewest not what scripture was, nor faith, but We made it a Light whereby we guide whomsoever We will among our servants. Truly, thou dost guide unto a straight Path.**[72] That is, you did not know what the Book was or the faith, except through God. However, God made your heart as a Light by which the reality of things may be discovered.

The beginning stage is thus spiritual wayfaring and ascension until you come to know God through God. Then the return is

---

71   Q Taghābun 64:6.
72   Q Shūrā 42:52.

direct knowledge of things through God, as in the tradition, "Dear God, show us things as they are." Your knowledge is of no use to you unless you have a Light in your heart, and it is through it that you will find guidance in the heavens and the earth.

You should know, moreover, that if you are in a state of invocation and something appears to you, the thing that you see and witness is not from your world, for otherwise someone else would see it just as you see it. This does not imply the joining of two distinct things. Rather, there are intangible subtleties which go and come to naught, and undergo transformation, and within their locus they inhere in other tangible realities. Hence the invoker may be in a state of direct witnessing of the cosmos which then becomes effaced in his gaze so that he witnesses other things. Thus they pass away into realities that are higher than them, without leaving any void in their place when they pass away. Rather, other intangible realities are configured in their place and come to occupy their locus. The cosmos in itself and through itself is changing with every blink of an eye, and is created anew.

The gnostic ascends in the chain of annihilations in order to return back to his primordial disposition. The wayfarer thinks that he is wayfaring forward, whereas in fact he is returning back, because everything that is unveiled to you in the worlds of the physical, spiritual, and invincible existed in the beginning. The wayfarer thus passes away in God's act first and attains piety and renunciation, then passes away in God's will and power until he sees himself to be powerless, and has a direct taste of the reality of trust and deference to God. Then he passes away in the attribute of knowledge by becoming extinguished in the knowledge of the Real, and tastes the station of surrender (*taslīm*). Then his existence passes away completely in God's existence until he has no existence in himself or through himself. That is the station of singularity (*fardānīya*), and it is an expression of annihilation in God's unity; and this is the Hidden *Alif*.

7.

The First Intellect
(*al-ʿAql al-Awwal*)

Mudhākara from the Friday
Gathering of 2nd Rabīʿ al-Thānī 1436/23rd January 2015

Bismillāh al-Raḥmān al-Raḥīm

Know, may God assist you with the holy spirit, that divine knowledge engulfs all things, and that the knowledge of the Real descended into the presence of prophethood wherein is the station of the first intellect, which is the disclosure-site of the manifestation of divine knowledge. This station has many names due to its exalted noble status. Some have called it the supreme tablet (*al-lawḥ al-ʿaẓīm*), the soul of prophethood (*nafs al-nubūwa*), or the supreme spirit (*al-rūḥ al-aʿzam*), which is the kernel of the original spirit (*lubb al-rūḥ al-aṣlī*). Thus, for the sake of self-purification (*tazkīya*), whenever your lower self tells you that you possess knowledge or understanding because your tiny intellect encompasses something, you must return to the realization of your original reality which is ignorance, that God may extend to you some of His knowledge.

Thus, the prophetic intellect is the intermediary that mediates the very starting point of existence, because there must necessarily be a spatial intermediary in order for receptivity and transmission (*talaqqī* and *ilqā'*) to take place. Just so, in the noble prophetic biography, the Beloved ﷺ used to take from the intermediacy of Gabriel. From this divine knowledge that manifested upon the Prophet ﷺ, authority over creatures is acquired, such as was manifested in the miraculous feats that appeared at the hands of prophets.

With regard to sainthood, this manifests in the form of the charismatic gift (*karāma*). And these are taken for granted at the core of the readings of the levels of the Name, which are called the rare readings (*al-qirā'āt al-shādhdha*).[73]

You should know, moreover, that the essential function of prophethood is not restricted to guidance alone and to establishing the lordly constitution that binds the believers, in order for them to be among the felicitous. Rather, prophethood is a sequential chain. Thus, when you hear that the Prophet ﷺ said, "I was the first of prophets in creation and the last in being sent forth,"[74] you must realize that his prophethood is the root (*al-aṣl*) that descended through the forms and presences of prophets, and that these descents are in the service of one presence,

---

73 Translator's note: According to the Shaykh's writings, the three rare readings (*qirā'āt shādhdhah*) of the divine name *Allāh* are learnt in the Treasure-Dot (*nuqṭat al-kanzīya*).

74 Ṭabarī, *Jāmiʿ al-Bayyān*, 19:23.

which is the presence of the chosen prophethood (*al-nubūwa al-muṣṭafawīya*), by virtue of their unity.

However, it differs within the realm of separation from one prophet to another, but it is all a Muḥammadan Reality. The secret of these descents is the multiplicity of perspectives, so that the unique emerald and the seal of the circle by which God opened prophethood and sealed it, may come to manifest. This is none other than the Master of Existence (*sayyid al-wujūd*), the one who praises (*al-ḥāmid*), and the one who is praised (*al-maḥmūd*), our liege and master Muḥammad ﷺ.

In the hadith of the intercession, which is a long hadith, God's Messenger ﷺ told of how mankind will seek intercession from prophets one after the other in order for them to intercede with God concerning their reckoning, due to how long they will have been standing without being judged for their deeds. This will go on until mankind arrives at Jesus عليه السلام, who will tell them, "Tell me—if there are some goods in a sealed container, can anyone access what is in the receptacle until the seal is broken?" They will reply, "no." He will say, "That is Muḥammad ﷺ, the Seal of the Prophets."

This Muḥammadan chain in the prophets unveils to us the full spectrum of dimensions and enables us to look at the circle or seal from every angle, in contrast to looking at it from one angle alone, which would grant us a deficient knowledge. Thus, if you wish to be a possessor of knowledge, you must be Adamic, and Abrahamic, and Mosaic, and Christic. For through every prophetic presence, you gain knowledge of the Muḥammadan

Reality in the measure of your receptacle, not its measure. You come to discover the purpose behind the manifestation of the levels of existence in the mirror of existence; and through that, you attain complete felicity through the effusion of sublime knowledge. For you have no power to discover the supreme spirit except by passing through its presences, one after another.

Now, dear disciple, you come to grasp the importance of the foundational principles of wayfaring which we have established for your journey. For you cannot bear all the levels of the names at once. Rather, you must halt at each one, station by station. You must discover the innermost secret from one aspect to another, until you complete what was decreed for you from those presences and those secrets. This is why when you recite the Noble Qur'ān through one secret, or one level, you sense an incapacity to understand it, because the Qur'ān engulfs and encompasses and enfolds within it all the levels and secrets. The more you advance in wayfaring and ascend in the secrets, the more you possess the keys to understanding the Qur'ān.

You should also know that true knowledge is knowledge of the Real. We only possess the flow of articulating it, by the secret of, **And say: My Lord, increase me in knowledge.**[75] This is because you possess a level in the celestial world, in the presence of God when He said, **Am I not your Lord?** and they said, **Indeed Thou art** (*balā*).[76] And right now, in the herebelow, you must train your soul in an all-encompassing manner in order to

75   Q Ṭāhā 20:114.
76   Q A'rāf 7:172.

regain the direct tasting of *balā* and of its enunciation.

You should also know that primordial knowledge is the knowledge of the Lord, namely knowledge of divine oneness. It is as if God's knowledge is a manifestation of the Days of God (*ayyām Allāh*); and nothing veiled you from the reality of His oneness except for your delimitation in time and space, which is why you sought to understand the speech of God through you, not through Him, and as you desire, not as He desires. This is why He appointed for you the *Kāf* of Divine Immanence (*kāf al-tashbīh*), so that you may sit upon the shore of *ka-annaka*, 'as if', in order to plunge into the ocean of *tarāhu*, 'you see Him'. Thus, the revealed Law is the gate to reality.[77]

Moreover, the revealed Law transmits the chronicle (*sīra*) of unfolding events and norms which are narrated by the first principle and accepted by the intellect deferentially and without requiring proof. This is the beginning of the entry to the exalted presence. As for the narrow intellect, it cannot expand its scope to perceive things that are unseen. It cannot bind anything at all, which is why it can fall prey to the suggestions of Iblīs and fall into his trap and into a state of doubt. Iblīs in fact usually enters through this gate because of his knowledge of the

---

77 Translator's note: This last sentence is a reference to the famous Hadith of Gabriel (Bukhārī, *Ṣaḥīḥ*, 1:15) in which the Prophet defines the three levels of religion, namely submission (*islām*), faith (*īmān*), and spiritual excellence (*iḥsān*). When asked about spiritual excellence, the Prophet responded: "It is to worship Allah as if you see Him (*ka'annaka tarāhu*), and if you see Him not, He nevertheless sees you." The *Kāf al-tashbīh*, of the "as if" (*ka'anna*) in this response, takes on a terminological and doctrinal significance in the Shaykh's writings.

delimitation and narrowness of your intellect. But if you place your trust in God, you will cast your soul at the doorstep of His bounty, exonerating yourself from all pretensions to power, and surrendering yourself to the authority of Lordship. Thus you will be delivered from the snares of Iblīs by your Lord, not by yourself.

This is why the invocation of God in wayfaring must be through the gate of the revealed Law, so that you may be safe. Those who invoke using symbols or talismans that they do not understand may arrive at a state where they can change the habitual course of nature, but without entering through God's Law. That is falsehood, and one fears for those who do so, because the divine secrets cannot be received except by entering through God's Law.

The first principle is the Light, and it is the supreme spirit. God says, **His command when He wills a thing is for Him to say to it, "Be!," and it is.**[78] A thing (*shay'*) is appointed by God according to divine norms (*nawāmīs*) that are firmly fixed and principles that are ordered. This is why it is possible for the knowers of God to unveil the innermost secrets of nature. This contrasts with those who arrive at the ability to change the habitual course of nature outside the realm of the revealed Law, such as the Dajjāl, who will have knowledge of these divine norms, and will be able to change nature, and at whose hands will appear supernatural feats. However, the marks of decep-

---

78   Q Yā Sīn 36:82.

tion and abasement will be inscribed upon his forehead, and his behavior will be demonic, because he will not have acquired his knowledge through the gate of the revealed Law.

Now prophethood, according to this approach, is knowledge that requires knowledge of the divine norms. This is why prophethood changes the habitual course of nature through miraculous feats by the permission of the Lord's command, such as how Jesus ﷺ used to revive the dead by God's permission, and heal the leper and the blind, and so on. They displayed these miracles before mankind so that they would believe in them. Thus, the Prophet is a knower of the divine norms (*nawāmīs*). Mastery of this knowledge enables its possessor to attain knowledge of the causes behind the existence of the revealed Laws, such as the reason for washing one's hands three times before placing them in a vessel. For when its secret is unveiled, there is a change in one's understanding and tasting. The same goes for all the rulings of the revealed Law.

You should know, moreover, that the spatial location of al-Muṣṭafā ﷺ, in the realm of outward delimitation, is the luminous city of Medina, in all its beauty, which is the radiance of this world. But in view of the inner dimension, all things, whether they are manifest to us or not, are created from his Light ﷺ. This is what becomes unveiled to the servant at the station of sainthood, not of prophethood; because sainthood [or divine friendship, *wilāya*] belongs to God, and the name the Friend (*al-Walī*) is a name that is shared by the Real and His creature: **God is the Friend of those who believe, He brings**

them out from the darknesses into the Light.[79] God calls Himself a Friend (*walī*), and He calls His servant a friend. A Holy Saying tells us that God says, "Whoever aggresses against one of My friends, I declare war on them."[80] This is why prophethood is sealed, because the Prophet ﷺ said, "There is no prophet after me."[81] Moreover, prophethood is a name that is ascribed to a created one but not to the Creator, in contrast to sainthood, which is not cut off because it is a name that is shared by God and by creatures as well. The Real is everlasting, and therefore saintly friendship with Him lasts through God's everlastingness, not through the annihilation of creatures. Sainthood will thus always disclose itself through some of God's servants in every age.

You should also know, dear wayfarer, that the Prophet ﷺ has an outer and an inner dimension. Outwardly it is prophethood, and inwardly it is sainthood. This is why the liminal position

---

79   Q Baqara 2:257.

80   Translator's note: this is an excerpt from a longer of a Holy Tradition (*hadith qudsī*), which reads: "Whosoever aggresses against a saint of Mine, I declare war on them. My servant does not draw near to Me with anything more beloved to Me than that which I made obligatory upon him, and my servant continues to draw near to Me with supererogatory devotions until I love him. When I love him I am his hearing with which he hears, his seeing with which he sees, his hand with which he seizes, and his foot with which he walks. If he asks me, I will surely give to him, and if he seeks refuge in Me, I will surely protect him." Bukhārī, *Ṣaḥīḥ*, 3:1319.

81   Ibn Mājah, *Sunan*, 22.

of the *Alif* is saintly, and why at the level of sainthood, the realities (*al-ḥaqāʾiq*) possess the station of existentiation (*takwīn*) and engendering (*ījād*). God has described to us in His Holy Book how singular sainthood (*al-wilāya al-fardānīya*) came together with prophethood in the realm of separation, through the story of the God's Confidant ﷺ (*al-Kalīm*, or Moses) and al-Khiḍr ﷺ. Now it is true that Moses ﷺ was at once a saint, a prophet, and a messenger.

However, God wanted to illustrate to us some of the realities that pertain specifically to sainthood and not the others, by way of manifesting its non-delimitation vis-à-vis the delimitation of prophethood. For had Moses ﷺ been the one who punctured a hole through the ship, killed the youth, and built the wall, it would have been said that he did so by virtue of his prophethood. Then the reality of sainthood would not have come to manifest, because Sayyidunā al-Khiḍr ﷺ was a saint, not a prophet or a messenger. At that time, he was a follower of Moses ﷺ. Now this does not imply the superiority of al-Khiḍr ﷺ over Moses ﷺ, because that is false. Rather, what al-Khiḍr attained was attained through the blessing of his following of Moses ﷺ. It is as if he was a Mosaic form that manifested with the property of sainthood, in order to illustrate the parable and make it easy to understand. And God knows best.

Sainthood, then, has the right to widen in scope to the point of passing away in the divine Essence, and this is when it displays for you the attributes of the Real, and your non-existent attributes come to naught. Your hearing becomes the hearing of the Real, and your seeing becomes the seeing of the Real. At that point, you learn the Oneness of the Real, through the Real not through yourself.

You should also know that prophethood possesses, through inner vision, two levels which both pertain to the higher part of the *Alif*. One of them pertains to knowledge and possesses knowledge of the esoteric realities, and the other concerns the exercising of control and existentiation, and it is what we call vicegerency. Both levels are brought together in the Muḥammadan Reality. Thus, it is as if al-Muṣṭafā ﷺ continues to subsist and to live, hence the mystery of his words, "Those who see me have seen me truly."[82] It is as if all those of his nation who are gratuitously favored by God and honored with a vision of him ﷺ, see him in the measure of their ability; yet the mirror of the Seal remains pure, a treasure that is unknown to its very core. This is because he is an expression of the disclosure-site of the Supreme Name of God and the Perfect Man. He possesses manifestation in sixty-three[83] allusions which are the foundational allusions of the Supreme Name.

You should also know, may God grant you success, that no separation exists between sainthood and prophethood. This is why we call it the Hidden *Alif*, and not the Original *Alif*.

---

82   Bukhārī, *Ṣaḥīḥ*, 6996.

83   There is a possible typo in the original Arabic text. This may be three hundred and sixty.

This is on account of the visions that are independently disclosed for each wayfarer. The *Alif* is Hidden for each individual wayfarer in a different way.

This brings us to the end of our gatherings in the presence of prophethood, which is a manifestation-site of everlastingness and inerrancy, by way of the station of the Hidden *Alif* through the *Hāʾ*-Reading. Nevertheless, in each presence that we speak about, and whose subtle graces we descend into the hearts of the disciples, much still remains to be discovered, for direct discovery of the presences differs from one reading to another. Thus, the presence of prophethood in the Hidden *Alif*, through the reading of the *Hāʾ*, is distinct from the presence of prophethood in the Hidden *Alif* through the reading of the *Lām* of Constriction (*lām al-qabḍ*), and so on. We shall return to it, with God's permission, in our other readings. As for this reading of the *Hāʾ* by virtue of the Hidden *Alif*, we shall enter, if God wills, into the presence of messengerhood.

SECTION II
MESSENGERHOOD

8.

The Messenger and the Messenger
of the Messenger
(*al-Rasūl wa-Rasūl al-Rasūl*)

Mudhākara from the Friday
Gathering of 9th Rabīʿ al-Thānī 1436/30th January 2015

Bismillāh al-Raḥmān al-Raḥīm

Know, may God grant you success upon the Path of sincerity, that we are entering upon the seventh station in the *Hāʾ*-Reading in order to study the innermost secrets of the upper half of the Hidden *Alif*, which is specific to the presence of messengerhood, which is wrapped in the shawl of everlastingness, and cloaked in the mantle of inerrancy. The possessor of this presence is not tarnished by any breach of oath, nor does he fall into error, because his knowledge is from God and is surrounded by God's attentive care, preservation, and oversight, in every movement and rest.

The knowledge of messengerhood has come in the form of milk.[84] It is worthy of the station of the Footstool (*al-kursī*)

---

84 Translator's note: this mention of milk is a reference to a hadith that describes the Prophet's nocturnal ascent (*laylat al-isrāʾ wa al-miʿrāj*). In

because it is the disclosure-site of the command and prohibition. It is identical with the station of lawgiving (*tashri'*), and it is a divine designation that is fixed and cannot be acquired. It affirms God's attribute of speech, because a messenger conveys what was told to him when he is told to 'say' (*qul*). This does not apply to everything he conveys, for when he conveys what occurs to his soul by way of incoming thoughts or inspirations, we would not say that he is acting as a messenger in that particular regard. Rather, that is a different station. God says, **O Messenger, convey that which has been sent down unto thee from thy Lord; and if thou dost not, thou will not have conveyed His Message. And God will protect thee from mankind; surely God guides not disbelieving people.**[85] Accordingly, messengerhood is that with which a messenger is sent, comprising divine pre-eternal speech, and what he is commanded to convey through divine authority. This is why we say that it comes to an end when the conveying of it comes to an end.

The messenger may receive this message through the intermediacy of the Holy Spirit who inspires it in his heart. To this effect, the Prophet ﷺ said, "The Holy Spirit has blown into my heart that a soul shall not die until its provision has been

one incident, the Prophet is offered two cups to drink from, one with milk and the other with wine. Upon choosing the milk, the Archangel Gabriel comments, "Praise be to God who guided you to the innate disposition (*fiṭra*). Had you taken the wine, your nation would have gone astray." Bukhārī, *Ṣaḥīḥ*, 679-680.

85   Q Māʾida 5:67.

expended, so fear God, and ask for plenitude in your requests, and let not the slowness of the provision cause you to ask Him while being disobedient to Him, for that which is with God can only be earned through obedience."[86] Alternatively, the message would reach him by way of an angel, which was the most common, as well as by other forms. A hadith of 'Ā'isha, the Mother of the Believers, states that "Al-Ḥārith b. Hishām ⁕ asked the Messenger of God ⁕, 'O Messenger of God, how does the divine revelation come to you?' He ⁕ replied, 'Sometimes it is revealed like the ringing of a bell, which is the hardest of all; and after that state passes, I remember what was revealed. Sometimes the angel comes in the form of a man and speaks to me, and I remember everything he says.'". And 'Ā'isha said, "I saw the Prophet ⁕ receiving revelation on a very cold day, and noticed sweat dropping from his forehead by the time it had passed."[87]

The Messenger would also receive revelation through conversing with God directly from behind a veil. According to Mu'ādh b. Jabal, the Prophet ⁕ said, "My Lord came to me in the most beautiful form and placed His hands between my shoulders, and I felt the coldness of His fingertips upon my breast. He disclosed to me everything in the heavens and upon the earth, and I came to know it directly. Then He said, 'Muḥammad, do you know what the higher assembly disputes over?' I said, 'No, My Lord.' The third time He said, 'Muḥam-

86   Ibn Abī Shaybah, *Muṣannaf* 7:97.
87   Bukhārī, *Ṣaḥīḥ*, 1:2-3.

mad, do you know what the higher assembly disputes over?' I said, 'Yes over the levels (*al-darajāt*) and the expiations (*kaf-fārāt*).' He said, 'What are the levels?' I said 'Feeding the poor, and prayer by night while the people are asleep.' He said, 'You have spoken the truth.' Then He said, 'What are the expiations?' I said, 'Performing the ablutions on cold mornings, and praying following a prayer, and dragging one's feet to the Friday prayer.' He said, 'You have spoken the truth.'"[88]

This revelation is not received by anyone other than the Messenger. Other types of reception (*talaqqī*) may occur to non-messengers; for instance, an angel may speak to a non-messenger, though we do not call that person a messenger. The Prophet ﷺ said, "In the communities that came before you, there were people who were spoken to (sing. *muḥaddath*). If there were to be a *muḥaddath* in my nation, it would be 'Umar."[89]

You should also know that a prophet and a messenger differ insofar as a prophet can only be a human being, while a messenger can be an angel. God says, **God chooses messengers from among the angels and from among mankind. Truly God is Hearing, Seeing.**[90] Moreover, neither prophethood nor messengerhood are in women. The prophet and the messenger concur insofar as both receive the revelation of a Law. However, the messenger's revealed Law is new, whereas the Prophet follows the revealed Law of a messenger before him. A prophet is

88 Abū Dāwūd, *Sunan*, 2:652-653.
89 Bukhārī, *Ṣaḥīḥ*, 686.
90 Q Ḥajj 22:75.

one to whom is cast the pure meaning which is specific to him, but he is not commanded to call anyone else to follow him.

Furthermore, there are things that are specific to prophets that others do not share with them, such as continuous fasting, or marrying more than four, as is the case with our Prophet ﷺ. Furthermore, all prophets and messengers were sent to their people specifically, except our Prophet ﷺ who was sent forth as a mercy unto the worlds. As for the heirs who are granted permission to convey, their chain is connected to God's Messenger ﷺ and they are also conveyers of the message of the Messengers. Thus they are messengers of the Messenger. This is with respect to the specific function of conveying the message. As for the general conveying of the message, that falls upon every one of the followers of the messenger by virtue of: "Convey on my behalf, even if it be a single verse."[91]

You should also know that messengerhood has come to an end, but instruction (*ilqāʾ*) without law-giving (*tashrīʿ*) has not. It continues by virtue of the Muḥammadan inheritance, so that the innermost secrets of the Qurʾān continue to descend into the hearts of God's righteous servants. This is a spiritual casting of inspiration in understanding the meanings of the Qurʾān. And if they are commanded to convey the message, then they become like the messengers, obliged to convey. But this does not mean that they change the revealed Law, for the revealed Law remains ever unchanged. Its rulings are fixed, and its com-

91   Ibid., 683.

mands and prohibitions do not accept any addition or subtraction. The saint does not come with any new Law, but he does bring a new understanding. Remember this principle, because it will keep you safe from swerving.

You should know too that possessing an understanding of the meaning that is intended by God and His Messenger is the epitome of testifying to the truth and the unfurled banner of sainthood. It is only granted to a God-fearing servant with a pure heart filled with the Light of the Beloved ﷺ, such that he begins to receive the innermost secrets of messengerhood through the Lights of the Messenger ﷺ, not through his own self. ʿAlī b. Abī Ṭālib, may God ennoble his countenance, was asked, "Has God's Messenger singled you out with anything that others do not possess?" He replied, "No, by the One who split the seed and created human beings, except by an understanding that God grants to a servant in His book, and what is contained in this scroll. The scroll contained rulings on manumission, indemnities, freeing prisoners, and the ruling on a Muslim who murders a non-Muslim."[92] If you desire further clarification, we would say that these Qurʾanic descents only occur to a heart that is pure, purified, and elected by God, as per the description of inspiration of the casting of the spirit in the verse: **The Raiser of Degrees, the Possessor of the Throne, He casts the Spirit from His command upon whomsoever He will among His servants to warn of the day of the meeting.**[93]

92 Bukhārī, *Ṣaḥīḥ*, 1395.
93 Q Ghāfir 40:15.

You should also know that just as the Messengers bring glad tidings and warnings, the saint may bring glad tidings and warnings. However, they are not delimited by recompense and punishment. As for the messenger, he gives glad tidings and qualifies this glad tiding with a specific compensation; and this is only for the messenger. It is as if he establishes a formula which if you resolve, you are among the people of deliverance, while otherwise you are not. Or as though he gave good tidings to the unbeliever in his state of unbelief, and warned a believer in his state of faith, such as in the hadith about the one who killed himself during his pious warfare (*jihād*). This is specific to the messenger, and sainthood has no part in it. What remains for the saints is the attribute of measuring (*qudra*), so that he might say a certain individual is among the people of goodness, or has goodness in him, or that he has a great future ahead of him, without delimiting it to specific deeds. They know this because of a special disclosure that is given to them. This is from the prophethood of news-giving (*ikhbār*), not from the prophethood of law-giving (*tashrī'*).

Messengerhood is from the station of the Footstool, which is why it is specific to the one whose intellect has expanded. All the worlds, in relation to the Footstool, are like a ring cast into the desert. Consequently, the starting point of messengerhood is the Footstool, and its end point is the Lote Tree of the Furthest Boundary (*sidrat al-muntahā*). Sayyidunā Muḥammad ﷺ entered the Lote Tree through the station of messengerhood, and brought back the canonical prayer from it. Furthermore, the human nature of messengerhood contains many meanings. Sometimes it implies the meaning of servanthood and needfulness, and the negation of divinity. This is why God frequently emphasizes their human nature, so that one may not imagine anything else about them. God says, **The Messiah son of Mary was but a messenger; messengers passed away before him; and his mother was truthful. Both of them ate food. Behold how We make the signs clear unto them. Yet, behold how they are perverted.**[94]

Furthermore, messengerhood is the furthest end of the Perfect Man, which is why it has the right to return to the Lote Tree of the Furthest Boundary of "Be Muḥammad." It descended into a perfect, pure and purified form, and became Muḥammad b. ʿAbd Allāh ﷺ, by virtue of messengerhood, then returned through this form to the Luminous Handful by virtue of the sanctity of, "Peace be upon us and upon God's righteous servants" (*al-salām ʿalaynā wa-ʿalā ʾibād Allāh al-ṣāliḥīn*).

You should also know that the Muḥammadan messengerhood of al-Muṣṭafā ﷺ is the most perfect disclosure-site of the Real. For by virtue of the names, he possessed the disclosure of the all-encompassing name, *Allāh*. Thus God said with respect to him ﷺ, **You did not throw when you threw, but God threw.**[95] And He said with respect to him ﷺ, **Verily those who pledge allegiance unto thee pledge allegiance unto none other than**

94 Q Māʾida 5:75.
95 Q Anfāl 8:17.

God.[96] Thus he ﷺ possesses the innermost secrets of the all-encompassing Name specifically, whereas the other prophets possess the other disclosures of the names. Jesus عليه السلام for instance possessed the disclosure of the name the Powerful (*al-qadīr*), and hence revived the dead through God's power.

96 Q Fatḥ 48:10.

9.

The Station of Conveying the Message
(*Maqām al-Tablīgh*)

Mudhākara from the Friday
Gathering of 16th Rabī' al-Thānī 1436/February 6th 2015

Bismillāh al-Raḥmān al-Raḥīm

Tirmidhī narrates in his *Sunan* that Anas b. Mālik ⁇ said, "God's Messenger ⁇ said, 'Messengerhood and prophethood have come to an end. There is no Messenger after me, and no Prophet.' This dismayed the people so heavily that the Prophet ⁇ said, 'But there will be glad harbingers (*mubashshirāt*).' They said 'O Messenger of God, what are glad harbingers?' He ⁇ said, 'The dreams of the Muslim, for they are one part of the parts of prophethood.'"[97]

This hadith implies that messengerhood and prophethood were cut off with the sending forth of the Prophet ⁇, so that there will be no other law-giving but his. Given that prophethood and messengerhood are names from among the names of servanthood (*'ubūdīya*), since the Real did not call Himself by

---

97 Tirmidhī, *Sunan*, 2272.

those names, this dismayed the people because they felt that the connection between lordship and servanthood had been cut off. After all, a person is distant from God in the measure of his distance from his servanthood. Whoever is distant from his servanthood, it is as if he desires to share in God's names, but that is impossible given the annihilation of the servant and the subsistence of the Lord. This is why he ﷺ gave them the good news of the remaining glad harbingers (*mubashshirāt*), which are one part of the parts of prophethood. This is an allusion to his assuring the subsistence of the name *al-Walī* for us, the Friend, which God called Himself by when He said, **God is a Friend,**[98] and when He called His servant by the same name and said "Whosoever aggresses against a friend of Mine."[99] Thus, God assumes friendship over (*yatawallī*) His righteous servants insofar as He kept the name of divine friendship (*wilāya*) flowing through existence outwardly and inwardly, so that the servant may come to assume the character traits of his Master, as the tradition says, "Characterize yourselves by the character traits of God (*takhallaqū bi-akhlāq Allāh*)."[100] This relates

---

98 Q Baqara 2:257.

99 Bukhārī, *Ṣaḥīḥ*, 3:1319.

100 Translator's note: Although this report does not meet the standards of hadith criticism, many scholars argue that its meaning is acceptable because it is affirmed by a variety of other authentic reports and narrations and in this sense would count as being good in substance, or affirmed by external reports (*ḥasan li-ghayrih*). Many sound and weak reports invite the servant to assume the traits of God, and as such, the *takhalluq* tradition is used not as a prooftext but a catch-phrase to refer to this cluster of more reliable scriptural references. According to Qushayrī, the expression is found in God's statement to His

to the tradition, "My servant continues to draw near unto Me with supererogatory devotions until I love him." As for prophethood and messengerhood, they were lifted with the passing of the Beloved ﷺ to the Beloved.

However, the property of conveying the message (*tablīgh*) continues to subsist on behalf of God's Messenger ﷺ in this nation so that his message may encompass the entire worlds. The Prophet ﷺ said, "May God brighten a person who hears from us a statement, memorizes it, and conveys it to one who has a greater memory than him, so that the one who has a greater memory than him may convey it to one who understands it better than him. For many bearers of knowledge do not understand what they know."[101] This means that one who conveys the message from the presence of messengerhood does not truly convey it unless his conveying is literal without any corruption or alteration, increase, or subtraction. The one who hears or sees something from God's Messenger ﷺ must convey it just as it is. A different narration of this previous tradition from Ibn Masʿūd ؓ has: "The Prophet ﷺ said, 'May

prophet David: "Characterize yourself by My character traits" (*takhallaq bi-akhlāqī*) (Qushayrī, *Taḥbīr*, 310). This statement is ascribed to al-Wāsiṭī and cited by al-Sulamī in his *Ḥaqāʾiq*. The expression is also ascribed in various forms to a number of early figures including ʿUthmān Ibn ʿAffān (d. 35/656), al-Ḥasan al-Baṣrī (d. 110/728), Dhū l-Nūn al-Miṣrī (d. 245/859 or 248/862), Sahl al-Tustarī (d. 283/896), al-Ḥakīm al-Tirmidhī (d. ca. 318/936), Abū Bakr al-Wāsiṭī (d. ca. 320/932), Abū ʿAbd al-Raḥmān al-Sulamī (d. 421/1021) (Chiabotti, "Éthique et théologie," 170-177).

101 Abū Dawūd, *Sunan*, 3662.

God brighten the face of a person who hears from us something and conveys it just as he heard it. For many of those who
receive a message comprehend it better than those who heard
it firsthand.'"[102] This therefore excludes the one who merely
conveys his own understanding of something he heard from
al-Muṣṭafā ﷺ, because it is as if he were conveying on his own
behalf, not on someone else's, since attempting to understand
a text is one thing, and the text itself is quite another.

The Prophet ﷺ also said, "Let the one present among you
convey to the one who was absent."[103] The one who was present (*shāhid*) is the one who is in the presence of direct witnessing, and is commanded by the Prophet ﷺ to convey, just as God
commanded the Prophet ﷺ to convey. Thus he stands as a messenger of the Messenger ﷺ, and so he has a share in the name of
servanthood. This is why God pairs the latter with him ﷺ and
says, **Muḥammad is the Messenger of God, and those who are
with him,**[104] because those who are with him share with him in
conveying the message (*tablīgh*) of what they heard from his
noble presence.

And since the Real has sent forth His Messenger ﷺ as a mercy
unto the worlds, his message is a mercy unto all of mankind,
which he was commanded by God to convey in His words, **O
Messenger, convey what was sent down upon thee from thy**

---

102 Bukhārī, *Ṣaḥīḥ* 1768.
103 Bukhārī *Ṣaḥīḥ*, 105.
104 Q Fatḥ 48:29

Lord.[105] God also says, **If they turn away, we sent thee not as a keeper over them. Naught is incumbent upon thee, save the proclamation** (*al-balāgh*).[106] And He says, **Thou art not tasked with their guidance, but God guides whomsoever He will.**[107] What this means is that his ﷺ duty is to convey the message through the gate of messengerhood, and guidance is not his duty, because that is specific to God. God says, **Surely thou dost not guide whomsoever thou lovest, but God guides whomsoever He will.**[108] Thus, the Messenger ﷺ knew that the intended purpose behind messengerhood is to convey the message. He therefore did not hide anything from what he was commanded by his Lord. This is why God addressed his noble presence and said, **Were thou to obey most of those on earth, they would lead thee astray from the way of God. They follow not but conjecture, and they do but surmise;**[109] that is, do not listen to anyone's words, but convey the message regardless of what you hear from them, because you are the eye of certainty whereas they follow nothing but conjecture.

You should also know, may God send down the inrushes of His election upon you, that the most noble sciences are those which the servant attains by way of bestowal from the All-Bestowing. God says, **The All-Merciful teaches the Qur'ān.**[110]

---

105 Q Mā'ida 5:67.
106 Q Shūrā 42:48.
107 Q Baqara 2:272.
108 Q Qaṣaṣ 28:56.
109 Q Anʿām 6:116
110 Q Raḥmān 55:1-2

Thus, do not take its attribute except from the All-Merciful. When a human being reads the Qur'ān and understands it, he perceives the name the All-Merciful. And the one who comes to know the name the All-Merciful has knowledge of the throne-status (*'arshīya*) of the All-Merciful. And the one who has knowledge of that, has knowledge of clear speech (*al-bayān*). So turn to the All-Merciful first, in order to attain the innermost secrets of the Qur'ān, and so that the tongue of your spiritual state may open up and express itself through clear speech.

Beware of supposing that prophethood and messengerhood can be acquired. Rather, they are sheer bestowals; divine elections that are bestowed upon whomever He wishes among His servants. For during the time of the Prophet of God Moses ﷺ, there were those who were more eloquent than him, yet despite that, God chose him over all others, so that you may know that it is not acquired. There is no difference of opinion regarding this principle among the people of unveiling and inner vision. As for those who use their intellects as arbiters in this matter, without following a prophet, they have come to other conclusions, because the intellect sometimes hits the mark and sometimes misses it; and in the realm of unseen things, it misses more often than it hits. But when it halts within its boundaries, it hits the mark. This is why the revealed Law comes first before the intellect, and the intellect follows the revealed Law, not vice versa. God has clarified to us in the revelation when we should employ thought (*fikr*), which should always be accompanied by remembrance (*dhikr*), both with it and after it. For remembrance expels Iblīs and purifies the heart as well as the mind, and the servant is thus under God's attentive care, drawing from the presence of the Remembered One (*madhkūr*). When he hits the mark and speaks the truth, it is through God not through himself, because the servant has no power whatsoever except through his Master. This is why the intellect on its own is incapable of having direct knowledge of Lordship. So follow the noble revealed Law, may God have mercy on you, for it will guide you to the principles of wayfaring through the laws of this illusion until you reach the Lord Almighty.

As for the hierarchy among the messengers, that is not by virtue of messengerhood, but pertains to the secret of the individual messenger due to his special election with his Lord. This is why the most excellent in rank among them is the Master of Creation ﷺ, for all of God's messages come from Him in order to manifest the ways in which we are to interact with the laws of illusion (*nawāmīs al-wahm*), so that we may attain to the Real. This is why the pre-eminence pertains to the essence of the Messenger, not the message. Every Messenger has a secret that is specific to him, and by which he is preferred above others. The one who brings together all these virtues and secrets is the one who was granted the all-encompassing words ﷺ.

You should also know that the messenger does not necessarily have to establish a proof to the one to whom he is conveying the message. His message, rather, is compulsory. You must take it just as it is, whether you like it or not, because belief in the message necessitates this. Which is to say that you must follow even if you do not understand the wisdom behind the revealed Law. It is due to this secret that the followers are ranked according to the strength of their faith. This is why the Light of faith is cast by God into the heart of the believing servant whose heart is free from doubt, and who surrenders his spirit to God. It is an opening from God. This is why in our spiritual Path, upon the arrival of someone who desires to reach God, we give him the Light, because we see that the One who has guided him to us is the Real, and that the Real wishes that Light for him. Were it not for that, God would not have connected him to one who could bring him to Him. However, understanding and direct fruitional experience of the levels, and his state in them, goes back to the disciple himself.

Moreover, when a person finds faith in their heart that originates from direct tasting (*dhawq*), they will be unable to repel it. In contrast, when faith is based on proof and demonstration, it will only be as strong as the proof. When someone with faith such as this is faced with an obfuscation that falls beyond their ability to prove or disprove, their faith will be shaken. This is why when an idolater witnesses a miracle, their heart is softened; but then when an obfuscation occurs in their heart, the softness leaves them as well as their inclination toward faith.

You should also know that when a disciple sits and invokes his Lord, and then holy disclosures come to him, those disclosures are levels and pure meanings that are delimited in forms so that he may understand them easily. When he has a vision of these forms and disclosures, it is as if he is reading the title of the book. But if he wants its pure meaning, he must perceive what is behind the form. In this context, ponder the story of Moses ﷺ and the vision of God. After he heard God say, **You will not see Me,**[111] he was told to look at the mountain; that is, to look at the form. The one who halts at the form of the disclosure will have sound vision, but Moses ﷺ wanted the pure meaning and the root. **And when his Lord disclosed himself to the mountain, He made it crumble to dust, and Moses fell down in a swoon.**[112] When he passed away and fell down in a swoon, he had direct knowledge of the pure meaning and the innermost secret, and he returned to the form of the disclosure, then asked forgiveness from his Lord and repented. It is by way of this Mosaic station that the disciple follows in the tracks of the prophetic method. For the prophets were appointed by God as models to be emulated both outwardly and inwardly. Therefore, when the disciple halts with the form of the disclosure, he receives the "title"[113] of the knowledge, while the one who perceives what lies beyond the form arrives at the knowledge itself. It is as if when you are with the form of the disclosure, Mount Sinai manifests itself to you. However, its crumbling to dust is veiled from you. Thus, you must cast the Light of faith upon the form of the disclosure so that it may crumble to dust and come to naught in your witnessing, and so that

111 Q Aʿrāf 7:143.
112 Q Aʿrāf 7:143.
113 Referring back to the 'title of the book' above.

you may come to discover directly what is behind it, and the sciences and innermost secrets it contains. It is in this manner that wayfaring takes place.

You take the primordial Light of faith at the very beginning stage during your initiation (*bay'a*). Now in order for you to understand what we mean here, we will give you another example. The Prophet ﷺ did not look at the form of Gabriel ﷿ alone, but he also beheld what lay behind it with respect to the descending of the Qur'ān. For the intended goal was not Gabriel, but the Qur'ān. Thus, my dear disciple, the intended goal is the pure meaning, not the form of the disclosure.

Disclosures are not attained through thought; they come only from the presence of the Real. Thus, you must understand the message for whose sake God manifested the disclosure for you, because disclosures are silent texts, and you must decode their meanings through knowledge of direct taste. For instance, knowledge is a pure meaning that discloses itself in the form of milk.[114] Observe likewise your letters and your breaths which you produce through glorification (*tasbīḥ*), how they will manifest in the Garden, taking on forms. You will return to your furthest saintly aspiration, because when you enter the Garden, you will find there what you have given shape

114 Translator's note: this is a reference to a prophetic tradition. Ibn 'Umar narrates that the Prophet ﷺ said: "While I was asleep I saw that I was served a cup of milk. I drank from it until I saw it flowing through my nails. I then gave my remaining to 'Umar ibn al-Khaṭāb. They [i.e. the Companions] said: 'How do you interpret this, O Messenger of Allah?' He said: 'Knowledge.'" Bukhārī, *Ṣaḥīḥ*, 82.

to through your remembrance. However, the greatest cause of bewilderment are those divine norms which you emulated as per the approach of the messengers by purifying your soul and erasing alterities (*aghyār*) through the Light of your faith, until the innermost secret of your faith came to manifest for you on the Day of Increase (*al-mazīd*), when you will attain the vision of your Lord. This wayfaring cannot denied by anyone, because religion is divided into three levels. Sayyidunā 'Umar b. al-Khaṭṭāb ﷺ said: "One day when we were with God's Messenger, a man with very white clothing and very back hair came up to us. No mark of travel was visible on him, and none of us recognized him. Sitting down before the Prophet, leaning his knees against his, and placing his hands on his thighs, he said, 'Tell me, Muhammad, about submission (*islām*).' He replied, 'submission means that you should bear witness that there is no god but God and that Muhammad is God's messenger, that you should perform the ritual prayer, pay the alms tax, fast during Ramadan, and make the pilgrimage to the House if you are able to go there.' The man said, 'You have spoken the truth.' We were surprised at his questioning him and then declaring that he had spoken the truth. He said, 'Now tell me about faith (*īmān*).' He replied, 'Faith means that you have faith in God, His angels, His books, His messengers, and the Last Day, and that you have faith in the measuring out, both its good and its evil.' Remarking that he had spoken the truth, he then said, 'Now tell me about spiritual excellence (*iḥsān*).' He replied, 'Spiritual excellence means that you should worship God as if you see Him, for even if you do not see Him, He sees you.' Then the man said, 'Tell me about the Hour.' The Prophet replied, 'About that he who is questioned knows no more than the questioner.' The man said, 'Then tell me about its marks.' He said, 'The slave girl will give birth to her mistress, and you will see the barefoot, the naked, the destitute, and the shepherds vying with each other in building.' Then the man went away. After I had waited for a long time, the Prophet said to me, 'Do you know who the questioner was, 'Umar?' I replied, 'God and His Messenger know best.' He said, 'He was Gabriel. He came to teach you your religion.'"[115]

One must halt at these words in the hope of breathing in something of its spirit. Observe, may God have mercy on you, the direct tasting of 'Umar ﷺ, who is called al-Fārūq ("the discerner"), when he said that Gabriel sat directly in front of the Prophet ﷺ. He did not say "in front of the Messenger ﷺ," because Gabriel came in the attribute of a messenger, and the prophetic half of the *Alif* continued to disclose itself at that moment in the Beloved ﷺ, so that the *Alif* was completed through the meeting of the Messenger Gabriel and the Prophet Muḥammad ﷺ. As for why he came in the form of a man, it is because he came to the Muḥammadan form in the Prophet's mosque, may God increase it in honor. Had he descended to a star, he would have manifested in a different form.

So he said, "O Muḥammad, tell me about submission." He did not say "O Messenger of God" or "O Prophet of God,"

---

115 Muslim, *Ṣaḥīḥ*, 8. Translated by William Chittick and Sachiko Murata with some modifications.

because prophethood and messengerhood were already manifest and ontologically affirmed, so he addressed him with the name of servanthood, "O Muḥammad ﷺ." And they had that conversation between prophethood and messengerhood. Thus, the religion is not understood in its totality except through taking its three levels into account, and wayfaring through them. *Islām* is the practical side, *Īmān* is the site of belief of the heart, and *Iḥsān* is the site of the spirit. Bringing the three together enables you to attain the pure meaning of perfection.

10.

The Dialogue of the Names
(*Ḥiwār al-Asmā'*)

Mudhākara from the Friday
Gathering of 1st Jumādā al-Ūlā 1436/20th February 2015

Bismillāh al-Raḥmān al-Raḥīm

Know, may God assist you with His success, that the flow of luminosity and reception from the All-Merciful does not occur between the instructor and the receiver unless there is a correspondence between the two, because each genus inclines to its own kind. Certain souls acquire layers of veils and become blameworthy, and they perceive that the revelation only descends upon those who resemble them in form. Because of all this, God responds to them by saying: **Say, were there angels walking about upon the earth in peace, we would have sent down upon them an angel from heaven as a messenger.**[116] This is an address to those who refused to have faith in him ﷺ, who turned away from his Sunnah and his guidance, because they saw him to be like them in shape, sent as he ﷺ was in the form of a human messenger. They halted at his human nature and

---

116 Q Isrā' 17:95.

refused to surrender to his special election, which God made as manifest as the sun and its morning brightness. What prevented them from seeing the brilliance of his sun upon them was none other than the manifold veils that came to reside in their hearts, covering and concealing the truth. That is none other than the veil of witnessing resemblance (*mithlīya*). This is why God told his Messenger ﷺ to tell them that were there angels walking about in peace on earth, He would have sent down from heaven an angel as a messenger. For an angel can only be seen by an angel, or by one whom God makes qualified to see one. Given this, and given how humans are the ones who reside upon the face of the earth, God sent to them a human messenger. He was upon their form outwardly, but was elected by the Lord: **And I have fashioned thee for Myself.**[117]

The lower soul usually does not welcome the prescriptive command that is brought by the messengers; it wishes to take from other than its own kind, but that is contrary to divine wisdom, for we can only emulate something that resembles us. If souls were left to their own design, they would ruin their own welfare and corrupt their livelihood. The strong would exert power over the weak, and the rich over the poor, because of the variety of their desires and goals. We therefore need a chain that connects us in wayfaring back to God, one that organizes our wayfaring among us, and one through whose directives we interact with our environment. Hence the need for a messen-

---

117 Q Ṭāhā 20:41.

ger from God who comes to us with a revealed Law that organizes our illusory livelihood for us.

In other words, with respect to the presence of the divine names, it is as though the names are brought together in the presence of the Named. They seek to manifest their realities and to expose their entities in the non-existent realm of worldly traces and effects (*athār*, sing. *athar*), and they seek to have authority over this non-existing realm. When they were brought together before the manifestation of the trace, they looked at their attributes and properties, and found every name to be contrary to the other within a single divine entity. The All-Hearing is the All-Wise, which is the All-Powerful, by virtue of the singularity of the Essence. At the same time, the All-Hearing is not the All-Wise, which is not the All-Powerful, by virtue of the diversity of their ruling properties and requirements. This is why the names demanded of the all-encompassing name *Allāh* to bring their properties and traces into manifestation, and it responded to their request. Hence God gave them the robe of self-disclosure, so that they came to manifest their authority in this realm of non-existence.

Now with respect to union and separation (*waṣl* and *faṣl*) between the *Alif* of exclusive unity and oneness (*al-Alif al-aḥadī al-fardānī*) and the two *Lāms*, wherein is the non-delimitation of the names, that which belongs to the upper part pertains to the realm of beauty (*jamāl*), and the lower part opposite it pertains to the realm of majesty (*jalāl*). Now the notion of directional relationship here, of "upper" and "lower" is purely illusionary, because in the spiritual realm (*malakūt*) directions disappear. If the disciple wants to be in the kernel of divine oneness (*tawḥīd*), he must unite the names of beauty with the names of majesty, so that one does not veil him from the other.

With respect to the *Alif* of exclusive unity where the names are in a state of non-manifestation (*buṭūn*), or you could say wherein is the cloud of the names (*al-ʿamā' al-asmāʾī*), from which the names descend onto the level of the Hidden *Alif*, and are brought together in its reality, and that is between the Singular *Alif* (*al-aḥadī*) and the two *Lāms* (*lām al-maʿrifa* and *lām al-qabḍ*)—with respect to this, they are brought together in order to demand the manifestation of their properties. For the Hidden *Alif* belongs to the level of non-delimitation and does not accept any form of delimitation (*taqyīd*), yet the ruling properties of the names do not manifest except in the non-existent realm of the traces, which is delimited. Thus it is necessary for there to manifest a reality that is receptive of the exposure of the effects and traces of the names in it; and that is none other than the *Hāʾ*. Thus, the names manifest their authority in the realm of non-existence, and the forms of the non-existent created things are negated by virtue of the *Hāʾ* of Identity (*Hāʾ al-hūwīya*), yet are affirmed at the same time by virtue of the secret property of God's self-subsistence (*al-qayyūmīya*), by which all existent beings subsist. To this effect, it has been said: "That which has no existence in itself and for itself, its existence, were it not for God, would be sheer impossibility." In *The Aphorisms* of Ibn ʿAṭāʾ Allāh, it is said that the realms of being (*akwān*) are fixed (*thābita*) through God's immutability, and obliterated by the exclusive oneness of His Essence. Consider this illustration, which may serve to make this more comprehensible:

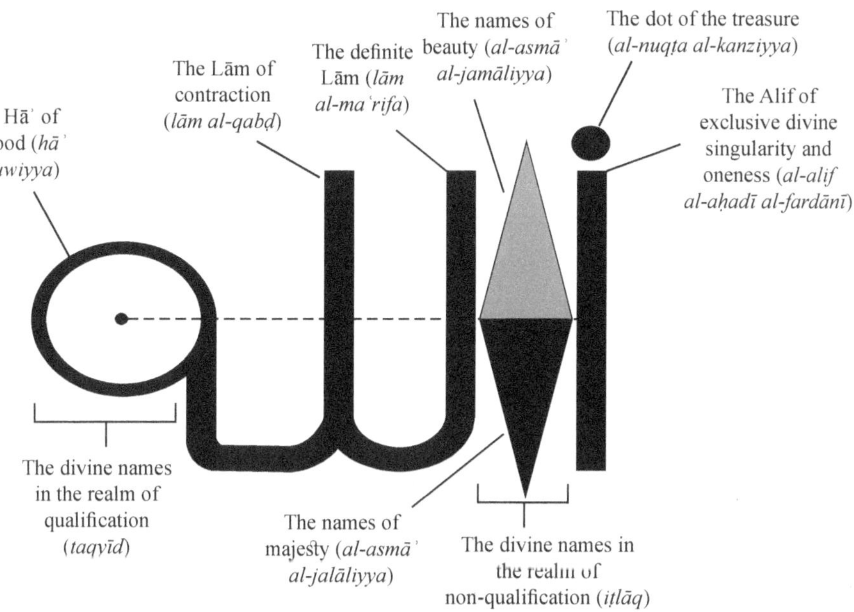

You should know, moreover, that the names gazed upon each other and found themselves to be unable to be independent of each other's realities. The realities of the First are tied to the Last, the realities of the Manifest are tied to the Non-Manifest, and so on. All the names intertie. This is why in our Order, one of the forms of deviating from correct belief with regard to divine names is when the disciple suffices himself with invoking only one among the beautiful names of God, aside from the all-encompassing name *Allāh*. Thus one must either invoke a name and its opposite, or add to it the name *Allāh*; for instance, *Allāh, al-Raḥīm*. This principle applies to the manifest names.

Now when these names gazed at the Hidden *Alif*, by virtue of their return to the exclusive influence of the divine name *Allāh*, they said with the tongue of the spiritual state, "What are we to do? How can we manifest our ruling and properties?" They came to know that the presence in which they were brought together would never accept their influence in any way. Similarly, for the disciple, when a vision manifests before him, he knows that it is not receptive of his influence, which means that he has no power to exert his influence in the realm of the physical, on account of his Adamic and delimited form of life. Or you might say that the seeker has no ability to bring down that which is in the spiritual realm (*malakūt*) into the sensory realm (*mulk*), or that which is in a state of non-delimitation into the realm of delimitation. It is from here that you come to discover the weakness of the seeker, because he does not possess the reality of the Hidden *Alif*. It is as though he owns a tablet, but no pen.

Now, when the reality of "Be Muḥammad" (*kūnī Muḥammadan*) brought into manifestation the authority of the names and the robe of disclosure, the non-existent forms came to manifest in the robe of needfulness (*iftiqār*), because they are needful of the authority of the names which bring them into existence. Thus, the Manifest caused them to manifest, and the Provider gave them provision, and the Creator created them, and the All-Knowing gave them knowledge, and so on. We too do not discover our true reality until after the disclosures of the names. Thus, the attributes of poverty, incapacity, ignorance, and all other attributes of servanthood, are inseparable from us. It is the names that took the request of non-existence to the *Alif* of exclusive unity, because prior to that, whenever they turned to a given name, they would find therein that its realities connected to another name. Thus, they found these names to be unable to connect them to the quest for the *Hā'* because authority belongs to none other than the exalted Essence. Or, in other words, we say that this is the station of the movement of non-existent repose (*ḥarakat al-sukūn al-'adamī*), because the realities of the names took refuge in the all-encompassing name *Allāh*, and found its presence to be the presence of union, and thus they asked it to manifest their realities. It is as though the all-encompassing name told them, through the tongue of its spiritual state, "I am the door through which you may enter into the exalted Essence." Thus the name entered into the Named; and the name returned to them, and with it, the name the Speaker (*al-Mutakallim)* emerged from the treasury of the Essence (*kanzīyat al-dhāt*) to give news of the commanding status of the Essence regarding the manifestation of the name-properties and the divulgence of their requirements, so that the realm of possible things came to manifest.

You should also know that when the realm of possibility came to manifest, the possibilities exerted influence over each other, by virtue of the variety of the realities of the names which brought them into manifestation. At that point, the possibilities feared that they would be collapsed back into non-existence as they were originally, when the names disclosed themselves upon them in their all-inclusiveness. This is why the one who invokes a specific name without permission is driven by it toward destruction, because he does not have an understanding of these regulating principles (*nawāmīs*). Thus, the first dialogue was for the sake of manifestation, and the second dialogue was for the sake of arranging this manifestation according to a constitution (*dustūr*). The names turned toward the all-encompassing Name *Allāh* in the hopes that it would guide them to one who would establish boundaries for them which they may use among themselves as a judge. The all-encompassing Name guided them to the name the Governor (*al-Mudabbir*), so that He may be a judge and a vizier over them. God says, **Allāh it is Who raised the heavens without pillars that you see, then mounted the Throne; and He made the sun and the moon subservient, each running for a term appointed. He governs the affair, expounding the signs, so that you may be certain of the meeting with your Lord.**[118] Thus the name the Lord (*al-Rab*) establishes the boundaries and the regulating principles in order to arrange the kingdom of names.

In light of everything that has been said, dear disciple, do not suppose that you will attain the knowledge of God's folk without striving against yourself, your caprice, and your devil,

---

118 Q Ra'd 13:2.

by stripping away all distractions and by wayfaring according to the revealed Muḥammadan Law. Otherwise you will be rejected, for the divine inrushes come in accordance with the preparedness of the servant and his saintly aspiration. As the Shaykh of our Shaykh Sayyidī Aḥmad ʿAlawī said, "Strive and you will witness" (*jāhid tushāhid*). Do not expect it to come to you in a simple and easy manner. God says, **Those who invoke Allāh standing, sitting, and lying upon their sides, and reflect upon the creation of the heavens and the earth: "Our Lord, Thou hast not created this in vain! Glory be unto Thee, shield us from the punishment of the fire!"**[119]

So at your beginning stage you must invoke the divine Name much, especially the singular Name *Allāh*, as per the verse, **Those who invoke Allāh.** This is in addition to the other invocations and supererogatory devotions. Then you transition into the stage of reflective thought (**and reflect**); and when you arrive at, **Our Lord, Thou hast not created this in vain,** you will have attained the dialogue of the names. And after that is the *Alif* of Exclusive Divine Oneness. And then the reality of divine transcendence will become manifest to you, upon the carpet of divine singularity of **"Glory be unto Thee,"** and the knot of your tongue will be untied with regard to the names, not the Named.

---

119 Q Āl ʿImrān 3:191.

11.

The Mortal Human Nature
of the Messenger
(*Bashariyat al-Rasūl*)

Mudhākara from the Friday
Gathering of 8th Jumādā al-Ūlā 1436/27th February 2015

Bismillāh al-Raḥmān al-Raḥīm

Know, may God assist you with His success, that everlasting-ness (*al-khulūd*) means the absence of withdrawal and return. This is why, with respect to the prophets, it constitutes conveying the message and being truthful. When God desires to choose a messenger from among His creatures, He assists him with attentive care and complete success. But mankind has grown accustomed to regarding with contempt those whose habit of disposition is one of simplicity and humility. So when the Almighty chooses one them to be their prophet, you find that the intelligent people among them, who are upon a clean innate disposition, recognize that God has a most holy effusion that He bestows upon whomever He wishes by His Grace. God says, **His command when He wills a thing is for Him to say to** it, **"Be!," and it is.**[120] Therefore God has the power to prepare a human being in the blink of an eye, and to honor him with messengerhood. However, at this noble station, there are some who come forth and claim that to which they have no right. This is why the people demand that those who ascribe themselves to the station of messengerhood must produce proof thereof. Those to whom he shows proof and indisputable evidence (*bayyina*) know that he is sent from God, and swiftly have faith in him and affirm his messengerhood. They know that God has announced him among the higher assembly, singled him out, and granted him a level that does not belong to others of his age. They see him as one who has the ability to bring down teachings from the spiritual realm into the sensory realm, by virtue of his sainthood.

You should know, moreover, that messengers are appointed by the Real as intermediaries between the Real and creation. This is why they come down from their stations to engage those of lesser intellects in discourse. Such was the state of the Chosen One ﷺ, which is why you find that he addressed each one in the measure of the scope of their intellect: the poet, the merchant, the farmer, the elder, and the nomad. Likewise, in our age you find those who claim to be upon the just balance of the Prophet's Sunna, yet they do not associate with those who are beneath them. Such people are proved false by their own state, which unveils their pride and self-admiration. You must there-

---

120 Q Yā Sīn 36:82.

fore learn how to bring down the teachings and unseen matters that you have come to directly discover, to one who does not know them, in a manner that is understandable and clear, because this is the Prophet's Sunna. This is the share of the needful servant (*faqīr*) in the Hidden *Alif* at this presence. Discourse, initiation, and elucidation must be done in the measure of the intellects involved in them; that is, what is elevated must be brought down to the sensory realm in the way that is most appropriate for each intellect.

You should know, moreover, that the messenger unveiled a small part of the mantle of lordship to the recipients of the message, enabling them to understand part of the favor with which God graced him. They found the one who was sent to them to be a locus of divine knowledge and lordly effusion, which they could delimit with their simple intellects because his knowledge fell beyond the intellect. So they believed and affirmed him, and the messenger showed them the deeds that would bring them nearer to God, and taught them of things that God created in the realm of possibility of which they had no knowledge.

It is in this manner that the messengers were sent in each age and place. All of them were truthful in their claims, and all of them affirmed the messengers that came before them, and affirmed and gave glad tidings of the one who would come after them. This is why you must love them all without discriminating, for the teachings of messengers did not differ at all regarding the root, but only regarding the outward branches, as was required by time and place. Had they all been sent in one time and place, they would have spoken with a single voice, because the root is one. All of them stem from the Treasure-Dot above the *Alif*. God says in Sūrat al-Mā'ida: **And We have sent down unto thee the Book in truth, confirming the Book that came before it, and as a protector over it. So judge between them in accordance with what God has sent down, and follow not their caprices away from the truth that has come unto thee. For each among you We have appointed a law and a way. And had God willed, He would have made you one community, but [He willed otherwise], that He might try you in that which He has given you. So vie with one another in good deeds. Unto God shall be your return all together, and He will inform you of that wherein you differ.**[121]

The revealed Laws, approaches (*manāhij*), and rulings may differ from one prophet to another on account of differences in time and place, but the innermost secret that flows through the root of the branches is one. This is why all messengers were sent with specific missions, because they were manifestation-sites of this flow, with the exception of our Prophet ﷺ, who was sent with a non-delimited mission to all creation, because he is the very essence of that innermost secret.

Faith comes after the appearance of the messengers. As for those who do not believe, they are dominated by lust for power over their fellow human beings. Had God manifested prophet-hood within them, they would not have denied a thing; but

121 Q Mā'ida 5:48.

since He ennobled others with it, they do not accept it out of pride, as God says in His Holy Book, **And they said, "Why was this Qur'ān not sent down to a great man from one of the two towns?"**[122] As for the possessors of intellect and intelligence, they affirm and believe and are worthy of the verse, **God bears witness that there is no god but He, as do the angels and the possessors of knowledge, upholding justice; there is no god but He, the Mighty, the Wise.**[123] Note that God does not say "the possessors of faith," but rather "the possessors of knowledge," because a witness must only bear witness through knowledge, otherwise his account is worthless. Knowledge therefore precedes faith, which is why He joins the angels and the people of knowledge to Himself, by virtue of the knowledge which He casts through self-disclosure upon the angels, so that they bear witness to the Oneness of the Real. Now faith is an active affirmation (*taṣdīq*) that such and such is a messenger from God. On the Path too, if you have doubt that this is a truthful Shaykh, then you have no share in the spiritual Path, for there must necessarily be the intention of active affirmation (*nīyat al-taṣdīq*). This is what revives your soul, so search for it in your heart and plunge into its depths so that it will speak to you truthfully and tell you if you are among those who actively affirm the truth or not.

Know, moreover, that when the truth of a messenger comes to manifest, it is necessary to follow him. The first message that

122 Q Zukhruf 43:31.
123 Q Āl 'Imrān 3:18.

a messenger reveals to his people is "no god but God," (*lā ilāha illā Allāh*), which consists of twelve Arabic letters, each of them written with the letters of the divine name *Allāh*. Then the messenger discloses to them the sciences of the unseen spiritual realm in the sensory spatial receptacles (*al-qawālib al-ḥissīya al-aynīya*).

12.

No god but God is the Key of Existence (*Lā Ilāha illā Allāh Miftāḥ al-Wujūd*)

Mudhākara from the Friday
Gathering of 15th Jumādā al-Ūlā 1436/6th March 2015

Bismillāh al-Raḥmān al-Raḥīm

Know, may God illuminate your heart with His holy Light, that the first pillar that is brought by the messengers is the proclamation of divine oneness *lā ilāha illā Allāh*. It is an everlasting proclamation with no beginning and no end. The *Muwaṭṭa'* of Imām Mālik relates, on the authority of Ṭāhā b. ʿUbayd Allāh b. Kurayz, that God's Messenger ﷺ said, "The most excellent supplication is the supplication on the Day of ʿArafa, and the most excellent thing I and Prophets before me have said is, 'There is no god but God, alone without partner' (*lā ilāha illā Allāh waḥdahu lā sharīka lah*)."[124] It is thus the first pillar of conveying the message. Each of its letters is articulated from the interior of the mouth (*ḥurūf jawfīya*), and so the one who invokes it must necessarily produce it from their interior. Moreover, each of the letters lacks dots, as a sign of its abstraction from any

---

124 Mālik, *Muwaṭṭa'*, 72.

object of worship other than God. It is a statement that brings together negation and affirmation.

Now, if a negation occurs upon a negation, it is a negation. But if a negation occurs upon an affirmation, it is an affirmation. Divine wisdom has determined that this negation (*nafy*) relates to all created entities. God says, **Has he made the gods one god? Truly this is an astounding thing,**[125] which is to say that the statement *lā ilāha illā Allāh* only contains a negation because of how people believe in the existence of other deities. So the negation came to remove this ascription from them and to erase this astounding "thing" (*shay'*), **so that they would** inhale the life-breaths of "God was, and there was nothing with Him." Moreover, multiplicity is negated by the affirmative particle *illā* of *illā Allāh*, "but God," thus affirming that which is affirmed in the heart of the one who supposed other than that.

Moreover, the statement *lā ilāha illā Allāh* is written with three letters, namely *Alif*, *Lām* and *Hā'*, which are the same letters of the singular Name (*al-ism al-mufrad*) in which only the letter *Lām* is repeated, on account of a far-reaching wisdom. Its letters are twelve in number. God says in Surah Muḥammad (47): **Know then that there is no god but God, and ask forgiveness for thy sin and for the believing men and the believing women. God knows your coming and going and your abode.**[126] Therefore the beginning is through knowledge, and then comes faith in it, along with the requirement of following its rulings.

125 Q Ṣād 38:5.
126 Q Muḥammad 47:19.

You should also know that the key to the Qur'ān is the *Bas-mala*.[127] The number of its letters is nineteen, which is the same number of the verse that was previously cited in Surah Muḥam-mad ﷺ. If you take number nineteen and multiply it by twelve, it gives you the number four thousand three hundred and thir-ty-two. This is the secret of this noble verse. The science of this statement was sent down over a period of twenty-three years, which means that the Qur'ān, as a sum total, is the statement *lā ilāha illā Allāh*. In it the *Hā'* is repeated twice, the *Alif* five times, and the *Lām* five times.

If we take two thousand five hundred and fifty-five [which corresponds to the number of occurrence of each letter and its order in *Allāh*, i.e. from right to left: *Alif* 5, *Lām* 5, *Lām* 5, and *Hā'* 2, which make the number 2555, as seen in the diagram above] and divide it according to the number of the readings of

127 The *Basmala* is the formula of consecration and the first verse of Surah al-Fātiḥa: **"In the name of God, the All-Merciful, the Ever-Merciful"** (*Bismillāh al-Raḥmān al-Raḥīm*).

the singular Name, which is seven, this would give us number three hundred and sixty-five, which denotes the number of days in a year. This is why in our Path we enter into the levels of the names through the *Hā'* and not through the *Alif.* For were we to enter through the *Alif,* it would give us the number five thousand five hundred and fifty-two, and if we divided that number into seven, it would not give us the days of the year. This is why we must divide the circle into four.

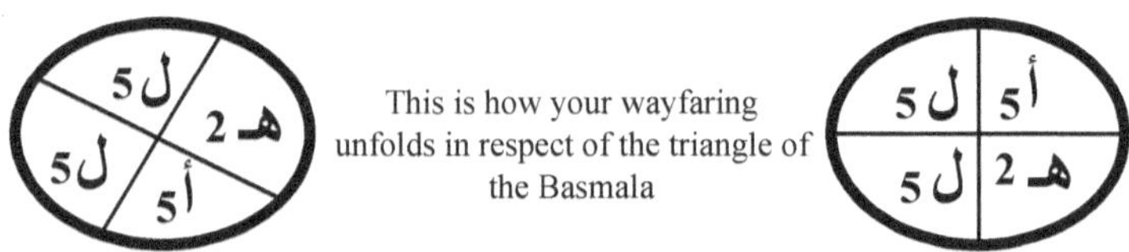

This is how your wayfaring unfolds in respect of the triangle of the Basmala

You should know that the singular Name has seven outward readings, and three rare readings (*qirā'āt shādhdha*) which are related to the Treasure-Dot above the *Alif.* This is because the innermost secret of the Name is enfolded within the heart of the servant. There is a tradition in which Sayyidunā 'Alī, may God ennoble his face, said, "Everything in the noble Qur'ān is in the *Fātiḥa*; everything in the *Fātiḥa* is in the *Basmala*; everything in the *Basmala* is in *bā'* and the secret of the dot, and I am the dot." This is why some of them have written the *Bā'* of the *Basmala* as if it were a *Lām* with a dot underneath it, like so:

Now we attained the number three hundred and sixty-five, which is the number of days of the year. Moreover, the seven readings part the veil for you regarding the seven days. God created the seven heavens and earths in six days, and there is a hidden day which is the Day of Increase (*yawm al-mazīd*). It is not one of the seven days, as some suppose; rather, the Day of Increase remains hidden and disseminated within all the seven days. The letters of *lā ilāha illā Allāh* are twelve, as per the number of the months of the year, and they contain the singular Name *Allāh*, which is composed of four letters with the *Lām* being repeated. We know that although the two *Lāms* of the Name resemble each other orthographically, there is in reality a great difference between them. These four letters of the singular Name are the four sacred months (*al-ashhur al-ḥurum*). In them beautiful deeds are multiplied, as are ugly deeds. There is a month which possesses the distinction of the Hidden *Alif,* in which all the secrets come together as well as the blessings of the four months. In the tradition according to Abū Hurayra ﷺ, God's Messenger ﷺ said, "The child of Adam harms me: he insults the aeon (*al-dahr*), and I am the aeon; I fluctuate the night and the day."[128]

Moreover *lā ilāha illā Allāh* is written only with three letters, which are the letters of the all-encompassing Name. No one can come forth with a sentence that is composed of just three letters. The singular Name is the most oft-mentioned name

128 Bukhārī, *Ṣaḥīḥ*, 2:1002.

in the Qur'ān, in that it is repeated two thousand six hundred and ninety-nine times. This is a prime number that cannot be divided. The numeral that is most repeated in the Qur'ān is number one (*wāḥid*). All of this is for you to come to know directly that God is the One, the Only, the Singular, and the Self-Sufficient.

So remove yourself and every object that is passing away from your heart, and then you will come to know directly the One who Subsists (*al-Bāqī*). This is why when the disciple is seated invoking his Lord, he should revere the Name, because by revering the Name, he is revering the Named. Abū Bakr al-Shiblī was asked, "Why do you say *Allāh, Allāh* and not *lā ilāha illā Allāh*?" He responded, "Because I do not want to ascribe an opposite to Him." The questioner said, "I want you to tell me more, something higher than that." He said, "I fear that my life will be taken away between the alienation of the negation (*waḥshīyat al-nafī*) and the affirmation." The questioner said, "I want you to tell me something higher than that." He said, **Say: Allāh, then leave them to their vain play.**[129] With this, the questioner cried out and fell down dead. His friends came to Shiblī, who told them, "A spirit was called upon, and it answered the call. What fault is it of mine?" The Caliph said, "Let him go. He is not guilty."

So when you invoke the all-encompassing Name you must stir within you an awareness of being in the most excellent of

129 Q An'ām 6:91.

days and the most excellent of months. You must be watchful of your breaths, of your clothing, of the space where you invoke. If you give great importance to that, the secrets of the Name will manifest to you and you will come to discover the all-encompassing month in it, and the all-encompassing hour in it.

Lā ilāha illā Allāh, Muḥammad rasūl Allāh contains twenty four letters, as per the number of hours of the day, and its innermost secret is that hour that was alluded to in the tradition of the Prophet ﷺ who said, "I have an hour wherein only my Lord encompasses me (*lī sāʿa lā yasaʿunī fī-hā illā Rabbī*)."[130] You must therefore search for this hour so that you can perceive the centrality of the Name (*markazīyat al-ism*) where the *Lāms* of Constriction and Gnosis (*lāmay al-qabḍ wa-al-maʿrifa*) are located. Therein is the hiding place of that secret, and the secret of the hour, and the secret of the months, and the secret of *lā ilāha illā Allāh*.

So you should know, dear disciple, that the key to supreme servanthood is to bear witness to *lā ilāha illā Allāh*. For it is through *lā ilāha illā Allāh* that the heavens and the earth are sustained. *Lā ilāha illā Allāh* is God's innate disposition upon which He created mankind. *Lā ilāha illā Allāh* is the first calling of the messengers unto their people. *Lā ilāha illā Allāh* is the word (*kalima*) of reverence (*taqwā*) and of submission (*islām*). It is the key to paradise and the abode of peace.

---

130 For a discussion of this hadith, see ʿAjlūnī, *Kashf al-khafā*, 2159.

13.

The *Alif* is the Foundation
of the Levels of Religion
(*al-Alif Aṣl Marātib al-Dīn*)

Mudhākara from the Friday
Gathering of 22nd Jumādā al-Ūlā 1436/13th March 2015

Bismillāh al-Raḥmān al-Raḥīm

The divine message is all the creedal directives and legal commands that God revealed to His Messengers for them to convey to the peoples to whom they were sent. This is the definition of messengerhood, whose source is one, whose goal is one, and whose furthest end is one, namely worshipping God alone without partner. This is why this station of the presence of the messengers and prophets is located in the liminality of the *Alif*. Nor is this arbitrary, for since their source is one, it is only appropriate that their station should be in the level of the *Alif*, which possesses the number one, and thus the one is in the one.

Now this vision of divine unity is the foundation that flows through the levels of the revealed Law. It is the station of the *Alif*, whose name when spelled out is itself composed of the letters *Alif Lām Fāʾ*, whose combined numerical value is one hundred and eleven (111), which is an allusion to the subsisting of all the levels upon divine unity (*tawḥīd*). We have here three ones, which comprise the *tawḥīd* of the beginning at the level of submission (*islām*), the *tawḥīd* of intention at the level of faith (*īmān*), and the *tawḥīd* of direct witnessing at the level of spiritual excellence (*īḥsān*).

Now submission is to follow the requirements of servanthood as per the Law that was brought by the messengers; faith is to voice *tawḥīd* in the unfolding that is specific to the deeds of the heart; and spiritual excellence is to voice *tawḥīd* by way of direct witnessing, that is to say, witnessing what God decrees and measures, hides and manifests. As for the most Holy Presence, it does not accept any addition of the servant, and so the one who enters into it comes to naught.

You should know furthermore that in the Qurʾān and the Sunna, God brings together the exoteric law and the esoteric reality (*sharīʿa* and *ḥaqīqa*). Hence the verse from Surah al-Takwīr (81): **It is naught but a reminder, for the worlds for those of you who will to go straight; and you do not will but that God, Lord of the world, wills.**[131] When He ascribes will to His servants in the verse, that is the exoteric law; and when He ascribes will to Himself, that is the esoteric reality.

Similarly in Surah al-Fātiḥa, **Thee we worship and from Thee we seek help,**[132] when God says, **Thee we worship,** it is the exoteric law, and **from thee we seek help** is the esoteric

131 Q Takwīr 81:27-29.
132 Q Fātiḥa 1:5.

reality. Whatever enables you to witness your deeds is from the exoteric law, and whatever enables you to witness the Real within you is from the esoteric reality. Thus you should not deny the knowledge of the inward (*'ilm al-bāṭin*) which is the esoteric reality, just as you should not suffice yourself with exoteric understanding of the law, but rather, you must plunge into its innermost secrets in order to witness things as they are.

Now the presence of the messengers ﷺ is a calling to rectify human society. This is why its revealed Laws differ in accordance to the time and place where those societies are found. As for the roots and the reality, it is one, and the center is one, which is the Chosen One ﷺ. This is why the Qur'ān is the most complete and all-inclusive of the revealed Books, and why all of the revealed Books are brought together within it. And this is why the Surahs of the Qur'ān possess this all-inclusive vastness. God says in Surah al-Najm, **By the star when it sets, your companion has neither strayed nor erred, nor does he speak out of caprice; it is naught but a revelation revealed.**[133] It is related that al-A'mash on the authority of Mujāhid said that the verse **by the star when it sets** means, "when the Qur'ān descends." And this verse is like the verse, **I swear by the setting-places of the stars, and truly it is a magnificent oath if you but knew, truly it is a noble Qur'ān in a book concealed; none touch it save those made pure, a revelation from the Lord of the worlds.**[134] The verse **your companion has neither**

---

133 Q Najm 53:1-4.
134 Q Wāqiʻa 56:75-80.

strayed nor erred is the main clause of the oath that is sworn in the verses preceding it. It is a testimony to the Messenger ﷺ that he is righteous, guided, and following the truth, not misguided—far be it for him ﷺ. For the misguided person (*ḍāll*) is the one who strays from the Path due to their lack of knowledge. The errant one (*ghāwī*), on the other hand, is the one who has knowledge of the truth yet deviates from it and seeks something else instead. God thus proclaims His Messenger and the noble Law to be far above the people of misguidance – including the Christians and the Jewish factions – and far above having knowledge of a thing yet hiding it or acting contrary to it. Rather, both he ﷺ and the tremendous Law with which he was sent reached the utmost rectitude, equilibrium, and balance. Hence the verse, **nor does he speak out of caprice**; that is, he does not say anything from caprice or ulterior motive. **It is naught but a revelation revealed**; that is, he only says what he is commanded to say. He conveys it to mankind completely and fully, without addition or subtraction. The *Musnad* of Aḥmad and the *Ṣaḥīḥ* collections contain the narration of ʿAbdullāh ﷺ, who said, "The first surah that was revealed containing a prostration was *al-Najm* (53). So God's Messenger ﷺ prostrated, as did those behind him, except for one man whom I saw taking a handful of earth and prostrating on it. Later I saw him slain as an unbeliever; it was Umayyah b. Khalaf."[135]

---

135 Bukhārī, *Ṣaḥīḥ*, 2:1010.

Moreover, in His Holy Book, God calls his Beloved ﷺ "the piercing star" (*al-najm al-thāqib*), and calls him "the Light" (*al-nūr*), "the most unfailing handhold" (*al-'urwat al-wuthqā*), "the truth" (*al-ḥaqq*), the "straight Path" (*al-ṣirāṭ al-mustaqīm*), "the shining lamp" (*al-sirāj al-munīr*), "the guide" (*al-hādī*), "the foot of sincerity" (*qadam ṣidq*), and other noble names. This is why the disciple should know that when he turns his attention to God in his invocation and exposes himself to the divine breezes (*nafaḥāt Allāh*), and a luminous star discloses itself in his heart, let him know that it is the Light of the Chosen One ﷺ. If he strives further, he will come to know that it is the unfailing handhold. If he strives further, as per the readings and the levels, he will know that it is the straight Path. However, if he turns away, let him know that it will testify against him; so beware, may God have mercy on you.

So long as this piercing star is in your heart, you must struggle against your soul and impose righteous deeds upon it, because the Path is made shorter for those who strive. Don't hear my words and fall asleep, but rather turn those words into deeds. Do not imagine that you will attain the spiritual opening, or proximity to God, or direct knowledge of Him, without courtesy and without deeds. For the perfected wayfarers are those who strive against themselves, because the lover can only arrive at his Beloved through the attribute of struggle. The true disciple is the one who comes to have direct knowledge of God, and yearns for His beauty, and wishes for nothing other than the Face of God. The way to enter into the garden of the yearners begins with the guide. When God guides your heart and brings you out from the darkness into the piercing Light, proper courtesy is to sit at the foot (*al-qadam*) so that you may attain direct knowledge of pre-eternity (*al-qidam*). Thus the one who does not have direct knowledge of God in this world, and does not experience the pleasure of divine proximity, will not know Him directly in the hereafter and will not experience the pleasure of the beatific vision. God says, **And whosoever was blind in this life will be blind in the hereafter, and further astray.**[136]

So if you have a piercing star, that is good news for you on the Day of Resurrection; and if you have a resplendent planet, that is good news for you on the Day of Resurrection. But you must work, and then come to know and have direct tasting, because the Light of the Real is only known directly by those who stay up at night. Have you been sincere in your companionship with the Light? Have you been its companion through love and rapture? Or is it that after that you had a glimpse of the Light, you turned away until the remembrance of God became heavy upon your tongues?

Do not imagine that the Hidden *Alif* is a line that you draw. Rather, it is a trace that you follow: **This indeed is my Path made straight, so follow it and do not follow [other] ways, for you will be separated from His way. This has He instructed you, that you may become righteous;**[137] so that you may return through the dot back to its root: "I am the dot."

136 Q Isrā' 17:72.
137 Q An'ām 6:153.

You should also know that the sanctified souls (*al-nufūs al-qudsīya*) are one, and that individual souls only differ due to the diversity of bodily constitutions. The Light is one, but its vision is diverse for those who witness it; that is to say, its trace in the body is diverse. That is why there is diversity in preparednesses; the water is one, but it differs in accordance with the nature of the place where it flows. The knowers of God are diverse in their essences, and thus they are diverse in their tasting.

Likewise, seeing the Light is a realization of the verse, **A messenger has come to you from yourselves.**[138] Therefore it is incumbent to revere it in the most superlative sense, because you cannot travel to God except through the names of His Beloved 變; and to the extent that these names disclose themselves to you, you come closer to the reality of drawing from the gushing spring of his prophethood and messengerhood until you arrive at the Creator, Glory be unto Him.

The lover (*al-ʿāshiq*) does not turn to God only when trials become severe, or only when he wishes to fulfill a worldly need. Rather, the lover is the one upon whom the state of passionate love (*ʿishq*) is constantly disclosing itself in his demeanor, actions, and words. Whenever his tongue moves, it moves in accordance with the speech of his Beloved 變.

Finally, since the *Alif* is composed of three ones—111—the question remains: where is the root that connects these three

---

138 Q Tawba 9:128.

ones? Here the tongue is incapable of expression, and drowns in an ocean of bewilderment, because none knows their root except the one who becomes a shadow of the reality of, "The hearts of the children of Adam are all between two of the fingers of the All-Merciful, like one heart."[139]

139 Muslim, *Ṣaḥīḥ*, 2:1123.

SECTION III
SAINTHOOD

14.

The Saint is the Treasure (*al-Walī Huwa al-Kanz*)

Mudhākara from the Friday
Gathering of 29th Jumādā al-Ūlā 1436/20th March 2015

Bismillāh al-Raḥmān al-Raḥīm

Know, dear seeker, may you be guided by the Almighty, that the presence of sainthood in the Hidden *Alif* possesses the liminal position (*barzakhīya*). Its affair is vast and has no boundaries. God says, **A garden whose breadth is the heavens and the earth.**[140] He mentioned the breadth but did not specify the length, but each one of God's folk has spoken about it in a different way. Yet none of them differ concerning the root of the presence, but only its particulars, according the measure of the differences of their own receptacles. The reason we started to unveil some of the realities of this presence was a question that I was asked by one of the Algerian disciples concerning the well-known tradition, "I was a hidden treasure, and I loved

---

140 Q Āl ʿImrān 3:133.

to be known, so I created creation and they came to know Me through Me." I had raised this subject during the Wednesday gathering, because that is the day when God created Light.

We say, with God's grace, that Imām al-Bukhārī narrated on the authority of Abū Hurayra ﷺ, "God's Messenger ﷺ said that God said: 'Whoever aggresses against one of My friends, I declare war on them. My servant cannot draw near to Me with anything more beloved unto Me than that which I have made obligatory upon him. And My servant continues to draw near unto Me with supererogatory devotions until I love him; and when I love him, I am his hearing by which he hears, his sight by which he sees, his hand by which he clutches, and his foot by which he walks. If he asks of Me, I will surely give him; and if he seeks refuge in Me, I will surely give him refuge.'"[141]

Another narration of al-Ṭabarī and Ibn Abī al-Dunyā on the authority of the Mother of Believers 'Ā'isha, may God be pleased with her, who states that the Prophet ﷺ said that God said, "Whoever offends one of My friends has incurred My war. My servant cannot draw near me with anything better than that which I have made obligatory; and he continues to draw near unto Me with supererogatory devotions until I love him; and when I love him, I am his eye with which he sees, his hand with which he strikes, his foot with which he walks, his heart with which he thinks, and his tongue with which he speaks. If he calls unto Me, I will answer him. If he asks of Me, I will give

141 Bukhārī, Ṣaḥīḥ, 3:1319.

him. I do not hesitate about anything that I do so much as I hesitate about his death. For he dislikes death, and I do not like to displease him."

This tradition is all-inclusive and all-encompassing in its definition of the station of sainthood. This is why it begins with a violent and majestic beginning, and its middle stage is one of wayfaring (*sulūk*), and its end is one of love and beauty. The name *al-walī*, the friend, is applied to the servant just as it is applied to the Lord. God says, **God is the Friend of those who believe; He brings them out of darkness into the Light.**[142] Thus the Godfriend, *al-walī*, by virtue of the Hidden *Alif*, is a treasure whose sensory shadow is enfolded within its holy Light. He is dazzled and cannot speak, like one who is overwhelmed in intoxication. His expression is incapable of describing his state, except that the intoxication of the drunkard is accidental and fleeting, while the intoxication of the saint is permanent; once it occurs, it increases and never departs. Thus the saint, before the sky of his intellect is rent asunder, gazes at the Luminous Handful and describes what he witnesses. However, when he plunges into it, he cannot speak nor describe what is within it. This is like the difference between one who enters the ocean and another who stands at its shore.

The station of the saint, then, is the station of inner vision and witnessing. With respect to the Hidden *Alif*, its definition is varied, as is our view of it. He is not the one who sees the Light

---

142 Q Baqara 2:257.

of God and journeys within it; rather, he is the one who loses his human nature and preoccupies himself with his Lord to the exclusion of everything else. For the *Alif* is one, and nothing is admitted into it except a pure fragrant breeze of the spirit. Thus, at the beginning of his plunging, he loses his created nature and is unable to describe or to speak.

You should also know that the people of direct witnessing have described the Light with different descriptions, such as the Handful, the gleam, the star, the planet, and countless other names. For these are the branches of faith, and the glance has been described in various ways due to the variety in the coloring of the receptacles. Direct witnessing is thus a fruitional tasting that cannot be described in words, because it melts the lover until it causes him to pass away in his Beloved. It manifests in the heart through direct witnessing, and in the eye through tears, and in the bodily limbs through emulation.

God says, **When the sky is rent asunder, and hearkens unto its Lord, as in truth it must; and when the earth is stretched out, and casts forth what is in it, emptying itself.**[143] This alludes to the sundering of the intellect that is incapable of perceiving, when the earth of the wayfarer casts forth what is within it, emptying itself of the tongue, passing away until all that remains is the divine secret that cannot be perceived; a hidden treasure.

---

143 Q Inshiqāq 84:1-4.

You should know also that if we calculate the letters of the word *kanz* (treasure)—*Kāf, Nūn, Zāy*—using numerology, such that *Kāf* equals twenty, *Nūn* equals fifty, and *Zāy* equals seven, the sum is seventy-seven, which is the same number as the sum total of *al-walī*: *Alif* one, *Lām* thirty, *Wāw* six, *Lām* thirty, and *Yā'* ten.

Hence, the saint becomes the hidden treasure, and this number points to the branches of faith as well (*shuʿab al-īmān*). The Prophet ﷺ said, "Faith consists of seventy-something branches, the most eminent of which is to say *lā ilāha illā Allāh*, and the lowest of which is to clear the Path of harm. Bashfulness (*ḥayā'*) is a branch of faith."[144] Now the word *biḍʿ* ("something," as in "seventy-something"), means a number between three and nine. Since sainthood is an ascension to the direct knowledge of God by way of the unveiling of the levels of the singular Name, it corresponds to the number of the all-encompassing Name which is sixty-six. If we add the ten readings [of the Divine Name] to the Treasure-Dot (*nuqṭat al-kanzīya*) above the *Alif*, the sum total gives us seventy-six, so that we remain within the range of the branches of faith. Thus the saint is the one who reads with the ten levels. And since the numerological value of the saint is identical with the number of the word treasure (*kanz*), this means that he is a treasure—seventy-seven—who comprises all of creation, the seven heavens and the seven earths. Thus he is both exalted and lowly; and

144 Muslim, *Ṣaḥīḥ*, 1:36.

the more the saint conceals his nobility, the more he increases in love, ascension, and proximity to his Lord.

Moreover, the abovementioned tradition brings together subtle lordly secrets and refined holy gnostic sciences. The hadith is well known on the tongue of the Sufis, and its meaning is sound beyond any doubt, even if its transmission has not been authenticated. The word *kuntu* (I was) in *kuntu kanzan makhfīyan* (I was a hidden treasure) is an ontological verb that does not express time, because God is the Aeon, and He is hallowed beyond time and space. Then in the work '*kanzan*', the *Kāf* denotes the *Kāf* of *Iḥsān*, the *Kāf* of "to worship your Lord as if (*ka-annaka*)[145] you see Him." Its number is twenty, which is the sum total of the twenty divine attributes. *Kāf* also means *katm* (to conceal). Thus you find, regarding the possessors of unveiled knowledge of the non-manifest treasure, which denotes complete incapacity, that their knowledge cannot be encompassed by verbal expression nor expressed by allusion, but remains concealed. Then the *Nūn* is the *Nūn* of *nīya*, intention, which must be detached and devoted to the Face of God, because wayfaring is based upon it. As for the Zāy, it denotes *zakāt*, which means the purification of the soul (*tazkīya al-nafs*) so that it may be cleansed and ascend to the highest degrees (*'illīyīn*), where it will be between the Hands of its Lord, pleasing and well-pleased. At that point the servant has a share in the disclosure of the name *al-Walī*, the Friend. For God says, **God is**

---

145 See footnote 77 for a discussion of the *Kāf* of *Iḥsān*.

the Friend of those who believe,[146] and thus God is the Friend. When the servant realizes the seventy-seven branches of faith, he ascends to the station of spiritual excellence (*iḥsān*) and comes to perceive the treasure of the Real, which is sainthood.

As for his saying "through Me they came to recognize Me" (*fa-bī ʿarafūnī*), it means that through the love of God, creatures came to have direct knowledge of their Lord. For love precedes direct knowledge of God (*maʿrifa*), and this love is none other than the supreme mercy and greatest favor, our lord and our master the Messenger of God ﷺ. When he says "*fa-bī*" the *Fāʾ* is eighty, the *Bāʾ* two, and the *Yāʾ* ten, which equals ninety-two. That is also the sum total of the word Muḥammad ﷺ: *Mīm* forty, *Ḥāʾ* eight, *Mīm* forty, and *Dāl* four. This means, "through Muḥammad they came to know Me," because he holds the reins of the seven primordial souls.

Each soul has its sky, and each sky has its treasures which emerge and come to manifest after the sundering (*al-inshiqāq*). When the heaven of your heart is rent asunder and is like a crimson rose (*wardatan kaʾl-dihān*) then it is forbidden for you to turn to anything other than God.[147] When that happens, the Reality of Realities (*ḥaqīqat al-ḥaqāʾiq*) will begin to manifest to you, so lay your nest in its midst in order to gain God's good-pleasure.

---

146 Q Baqara 2:257.

147 Here the Shaykh is referring to the verse **"When the sky shall be rent asunder and when it shall be like a crimson rose."** (*Fa-idhā inshaqqat al-samāʾ fa-kānat wardatan kaʾl-dihān*) Q Raḥmān 55:37.

15.

The Sainthood of Faith
and the Sainthood of Gnosis
(*Wilāyat al-Īmān wa-Wilāyat al-ʿIrfān*)

Mudhākara from the Friday
Gathering of 6th Jumādā al-Thāniya 1436/27th March 2015

Bismillāh al-Raḥmān al-Raḥīm

Know, dear disciple, that sainthood is rulership, authority, and leadership (*imāra, sulṭa, rīyāsa*). It is to exercise total control over creation through God, because it is the shadow of prophethood, and it is also love in its deepest sense. Its scope is vast and cannot be delimited. Sainthood is the realization of the dot of the *Bāʾ* of the *Basmala*. It is related that Sayyidunā ʿAlī bin Abī Ṭālib, may God ennoble his face, said, "I am the dot," as if to say "I am sainthood." This is the dot that is ascribed to the totality of the names and divine realities, because it is through the *Basmala* that God takes charge over the servant who has realized the station of servanthood and upon whom His names and attributes have become manifest in both his knowledge and his state. He thus expresses the divine attribute of being during his annihilation in it, while subsisting through the Real.

Sainthood, moreover, is divided into two sorts: sainthood of faith, which is specific to everyone who has faith in the unseen;

and sainthood of gnosis, which is specific to the one who has direct knowledge through witnessing and who attains annihilation in the Identity (*al- hūwīya*) of *huwa* (He), then enters into the *Lām* of Constriction (*lām al-qabḍ*) of "*lahu al-mulk*" (to Him belongs the dominion), then ascends upwards to the furthest end of coming to naught in the centrality (*markazīya*) of the Hidden *Alif*, when the *Alif* is split into two, and he comes to know the sainthood of faith and the sainthood of gnosis. Or if you wish, you could call it general sainthood (*wilāya ʿāmma*) and particular sainthood (*wilāya khāṣṣa*).

Now general sainthood is inclusive of all believers. Abū Saʿīd al-Khudrī ﷺ related that God's Messenger ﷺ said, "If you see a man frequenting the mosques, bear witness to his faith."[148] As for particular sainthood, it belongs to the realized gnostic and is expressed by the hadith of the saint: "My servant continues to draw near unto me through supererogatory devotions until I love him; and when I love him I am his hearing by which he hears, his seeing by which he sees, his hand by which he clutches, and his foot by which he walks. If he asks of Me, I will give him; and if he seeks refuge in Me, I will give him refuge."[149] So when the servant yearns for his Patron (*al-Mawlā*) by rectifying himself outwardly and inwardly for the sake of his Master, then God befriends him (*tawallā*) and conceals his attributes with His own, and his qualities with His own.

---

148 Ibn Mājah, *Sunan,* 118.
149 Ibn Ḥibbān, *Ṣaḥīḥ,* 108.

You should know also that the sainthood of faith has its branches and categories, as does the sainthood of gnosis, and that the sainthood of faith is covered by the hadith "Faith is sixty-something branches, and bashfulness is one of the branches of faith." Or according to Muslim, "Faith is seventy-something or sixty-something branches, the most eminent of which is to say *lā ilāha illā Allāh*, and the lowest of which is to clear the path of harm. Bashfulness is a branch of faith."[150] Thus the Prophet ﷺ delimited the sainthood of faith into sixty-something or seventy-something branches. This means that the traits of faith do not fall outside of this number. There is no contradiction with regard to the number of the branches; in our Path, either number can apply in the sense that the disciple achieves realization and comes to recognize when there are sixty-something branches and when there are seventy-something.

As for the sainthood of gnosis, it brings together all types of sainthood. It possesses one thousand degrees as per the general principles (*al-ummahāt*). However, in terms of specific differentiation, it possesses seventy thousand degrees, veils, or stations. The last of these stations is the station of incapacity (*al-ʿajz*), of which Sayyidunā ʿAlī, may God ennoble his face, said, "Incapacity to perceive comprehension, is comprehension (*idrāk*); inquiring into the secret of the Essence, is idolatry (*ishrāk*)." Similarly, Sayyidunā Abū Bakr al-Ṣiddīq ﵁ said,

150 Muslim, *Ṣaḥīḥ,* 1:36.

"The incapacity to comprehend is comprehension." Therefore, the utmost level of comprehension that the saint can attain is incapacity.

Attaining the substance of a thing is to attain the reality of the divine command regarding that thing. This is why the reality is incapacity, and wayfaring within it has no end. Moreover, it is not possible to limit the divine attributes, and therefore direct knowledge of God yields incapacity with regard to the core of His Essence, attributes, and acts. Despite your passing away in Him and your subsisting through Him, you will not be capable of bringing together the levels so long as you eat and drink.

You should know, moreover, that particular sainthood pushes the saint to loving death, because it is the bridge that leads him to his Beloved. Thus, the lover of God dies and is revived with every blink of an eye. The wayfaring of sainthood (*sulūk al-wilāya*) is annihilation within annihilation, until you lose your own attributes and come to naught, and then the attributes of your Lord manifest upon you. This is why I tell you that the saint who has direct knowledge sells his soul to God, and God buys his soul from him. God says, **Say, "O you who are Jews, if you claim that you are friends unto God apart from other people, then long for death, if you are truthful."**[151] So observe yourself, O you who claim sanctity: do you love death? For the true saint is the one who loves to meet God, and you know that this meeting cannot occur until after death, whether

---

151 Q Jumuʻa 62:6.

it be the voluntary or the involuntary death. For the wayfarer, from the moment he travels the Path of sanctity, is dying and is revived. He is watchful of none other than God, and has no time to be preoccupied with his relation with his grave, i.e., his body, for his concern lies elsewhere. His Path is one of annihilation within annihilation, until he subsists with none other than God. He is not content to resort to anything other than that. This is why we call this presence the Everlasting Presence, because one cannot dwell everlastingly with one's entirety until one loses oneself entirely. This presence does not accept any addition, for it is Light upon Light.

The Everlasting Presence is bewilderment and incapacity. The servant does not enter it until every atom within him is illuminated by the Light of God. This is why the phenomenon of losing the body entirely in the centrality of the Hidden *Alif*, and the illumination of the veins and limbs, is the foundation of wayfaring. The Prophet ﷺ used to say on his way to the mosque before entering upon the King of Kings, "Dear God, place in my heart Light, and on my tongue Light, and in my hearing Light, and in my seeing Light, and behind me Light, and in front of me Light, and above me Light, and beneath me Light. Dear God, grant me light!"[152]

You should know also that this noble prophetic supplication is inclusive of all the levels of wayfaring and journeying to God. In fact, even the manner of its transmission and the

---

152 Muslim, *Ṣaḥīḥ*, 1:303.

place where he would specifically make this noble supplication, all of this contains allusions that are not hidden from the possessors of inner vision. For he ﷺ would say it on the way to the mosque, which is an allusion to the wayfaring that the servant undertakes toward his mosque which is his heart, for the heart of the believer is the house of the Lord. Yet not every heart is fit for this, but only the heart that is filled with the Light of God. The Prophet ﷺ made it clear that this journeying is undertaken through the Light that is cast by God into the heart, and then flows over his limbs and veins until the entire servant becomes Light without darkness. Only then is he fit to enter to the King of Kings.

The primary veins (*ummahāt al-'urūq*) reach three hundred and sixty in number, as per the number of degrees of the circle of annihilation. In order for all of them to become illuminated, you must come to naught in the central point of the *Hā'* of Identity (*Hā' al-huwīya*). That is to say, you must come to naught in the second secret (*al-sirr al-thānī*). As for the one who remains outside of the center, one fears that he will return whence he came. When coming to naught in the center occurs, the veins become illuminated. The Beloved ﷺ said, "God created a preserved tablet from pearls. Its scrolls are from red rubies, and its pen is Light. God glances at it three hundred and sixty times a day. He creates, He provides, He gives death, He gives Light, He exalts, He abases, and He does what He wills."[153]

---

153 Ṭabarānī, *Mu'jam al-Ṭabarānī*, 12:72.

The Everlasting Presence is where the divine norms descend entirely with three hundred and sixty, without any addition or subtraction. In order for this roaming (*siyāḥa*) to become three hundred and sixty for you, you must give great importance to the center, and you must behold this web like a house of the spider.[154] This house is the most fragile house because your body is in complete annihilation, and you must illuminate it with the pre-eternal Aḥmadan sun, so that you behold your veins illuminated and resplendent.

You should also know that each vein has a celestial body that is specific to it, and a qualitative trait that is specific to it. You must extinguish the vein of jealousy, the vein of pride, and the vein of self-admiration with the Light of the Real, in order to train your soul and to draw the qualitative trait and direct knowledge from each vein. You wish to be a ray from the niche of the one to whom God said, **Truly thou art of an exalted character,**[155] and so you must erase the darkness of the veins so that they become luminous, like rivers from the wellspring of the Kawthar of al-Muṣṭafā ﷺ. Then you may drink from wherever you wish. The saint is the one who perceives his soul to be nonexistent, because every dark vein within him has become luminous, such that Satan has no way of accessing him; for Satan grazes on the veins of darkness, while Light

154 This is a reference to the verse: **The likeness of those who have taken to them protectors, apart from God, is as the likeness of the spider that takes to itself a house; and surely the frailest of houses is the house of the spider, did they but know.** (Q ʿAnkabūt 29:41).
155 Q Qalam 68:4.

burns him. An authentic hadith related by al-Bukhārī tells us that the Prophet ﷺ said, "Satan flows through the human being the way blood flows."[156] We know that blood flows through the veins. So if his veins turn from darkness into Light, then the servant is following the tracks of Sayyidunā 'Umar al-Fārūq ؓ, about whom the Prophet ﷺ said, "O Ibn al-Khaṭṭāb, by the One in whose Hand is my soul, whenever Satan finds you walking down one path, he takes the other one."[157] Satan used to flee from his ؓ luminosity. The same goes for anyone whose veins have become mansions or gates of Light, so that his demonic counterpart (*qarīn*) does not have the power to enter them. Each of these mansions has its own Light that is a different color from the others, colors that are entirely different from those in this world.

Bukhārī and Muslim narrate a hadith from Anas ؓ regarding the Prophet's nocturnal ascent. It contains the following: "Then the celestial steed (*Burāq*) took me and we ended at the Lote Tree of the Furthest Boundary, which was covered in colors unknown to me. Then I was brought into the Garden, which contained domes of pearl, and its earth was musk."[158] Now when the Prophet ﷺ said "colors unknown to me," he said it to protect the listener, because the Lote Tree is the furthest boundary of shapes that take on forms (*tashakkulāt al-ṣuwarīya*).

156 Bukhārī, *Ṣaḥīḥ*, 1:380.
157 Ibid., 2:643.
158 Ibid., 1:74.

He described to us the Garden in a manner that we can recognize; but the colors that covered the Lote tree are beyond our recognition, so he was silent and did not describe them.

By way of summary, let us illustrate this matter with an example: when someone struggles against the axis of the vein of envy in God's spiritual realm, he must remain in a state of stillness in the center of the *Hā'* of Identity until he finds that his soul has no existence, and all forms come to naught in his witnessing. It is then that he turns towards the vein of jealousy and begins to invoke God until it is illuminated by the Light of God, and this disease is uprooted from him. When he returns to his sensory realm in the physical world of God's dominion, he will find that he is completely cured of envy. This is how to engage with every dark vein.

Moreover, during his circumambulation around the *Hā'* of Identity, when the disciple returns to the center he will find that his Light is refracted into seven upper lights, which are the seven heavens of Lights and secrets; and seven lower lights, which are the seven earths of worship and invocation. This is in view of the number seventy-seven, which is the sum total of the numerical value of the name *al-walī*, the saint. When he returns to the center of his own essence, the earth of the vein of spiritual struggle (*mujāhada*) becomes his earth, and direct witnessing (*mushāhada*) becomes his heaven. Whenever he enters into a vein, he feels the throes of death, and the vein that is illuminated replenishes him with sciences, innermost secrets, and Lights of many kinds.

The one who possesses the *Alif* is grasped by God Himself without the intermediacy of an angel. Concerning this, we have said in a poem:

> *By God, the death of the lover*
> *Is weightier than the death of the grave,*
>
> *So long as the death of the grave*
> *Occurs only once in a lifetime.*
>
> *Through You I die and am revived,*
> *During my rest and my invocation,*
>
> *Just as the Folk of the Cave remained*
> *As the time of the Aeon passed by.*

Consider this diagram as a summary of this lesson:

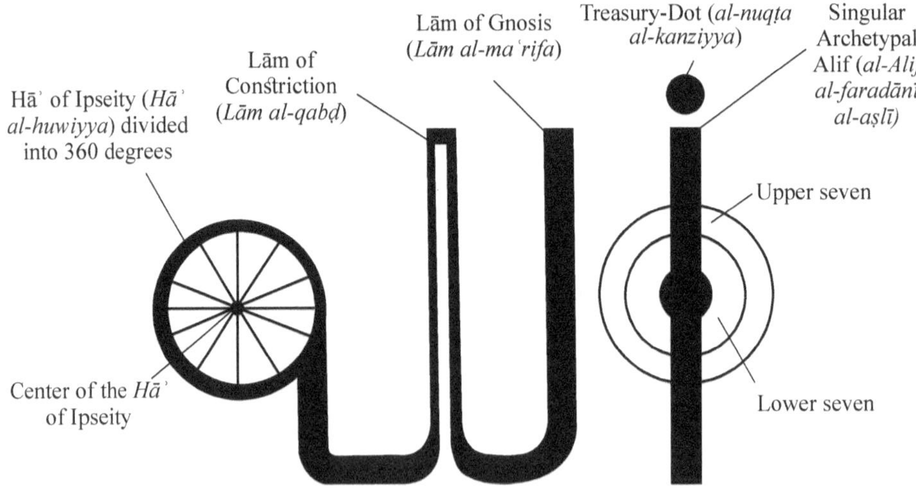

The total numerical value of the all-encompassing name *Allāh* is sixty-six, while the total value of the name *al-Walī* is seventy-seven. This corresponds to the number of the branches of faith, which fluctuate between sixty-something and seventy-something. Through the invocation of the singular Name, one plunges into the stations of gnostic sainthood in order to transform the dark veins into Light. This is achieved by giving Lordship its rightful due through total exaltation of the center of Identity, wherein lies the *Lām* of Constriction (*lām al-qabḍ*), so named because it is from here that the spirits are grasped (*tuqbaḍ*); and then by giving servanthood its rightful due, which is through invocation, worship, and turning toward the vein that you wish to illuminate and dispel its darkness.

Here is a diagram to illustrate this:

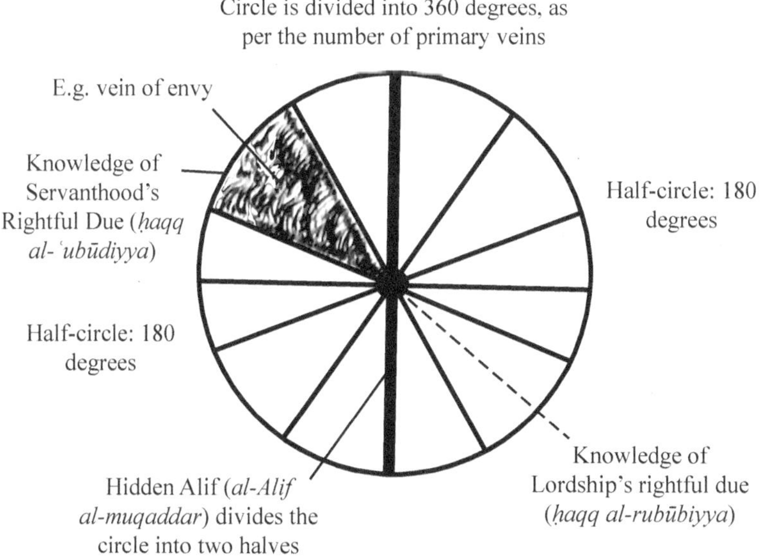

When you busy yourself with all the veins, one after another, you finally become a luminous servant who has come to realize the supplication that the Prophet ﷺ would make on his way to the mosque. The result is as follows:

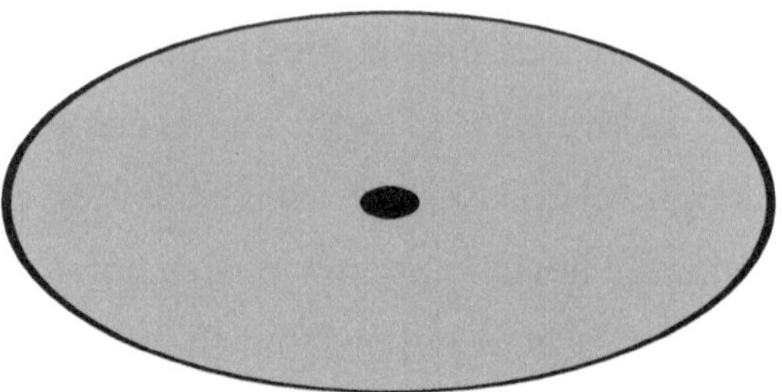

The circle of your veins turns from darkness into Light, and this you witness in the spiritual realm; and when you return to the physical realm, you find that your soul has become purified of the attributes of envy, pride, self-admiration, and so on.

16.

I Become His Seeing
(*Kuntu Baṣarahu*)

Mudhākara from the Friday
Gathering of 13th Jumādā al-Thāniya 1436/3rd April 2015

Bismillāh al-Raḥmān al-Raḥīm

Know, may God illuminate your heart, that during the last gathering we spoke of the Everlasting Presence in its delimited axis at the station of sainthood. We also spoke of how to rid oneself of the dark veins by making all three hundred and sixty primary veins luminous, such that the Light that is deposited into each one becomes a mansion. Then every vein takes on own special color and mansion that is different from the others in terms of its fruit and its Light. This is according to the hadith, "God created a preserved tablet from pearls. Its scrolls are from red rubies, and its pen is Light. God glances at it three hundred and sixty times a day. He creates, He provides, He gives death, He gives Light, He exalts, He abases, and He does what He wills."[159] Thus, God created a Preserved Tablet in which is contained what was and what shall be, and He told

159 Ṭabarānī, *Muʻjam*, 12:72.

us that it is created from certain created beings,[160] though its power and luminosity are more elevated. He told us that He created it from a white pearl, though the nature of this pearl remains veiled and hidden, such that we are unable to describe it through reference to created beings. And since God glances at it three hundred and sixty times from the realm of His command, and the number of the primary veins in the children of Adam is the same as the number of glances, we know that the two are related, insofar as these glances succeed one after the other upon the heart of the saintly servant. And once you discover the luminous glance which has no color, it refracts into three hundred and sixty degrees in proportion to the veins. At that point, each vein has its own specific color, its specific Light, and its specific fruit in which the wayfarer takes pleasure.

God therefore created a Preserved Tablet from white pearl, whose length spans between heaven and earth, and whose breadth stretches from East to West. The grasp of the intellect is enraptured in it when it conceives of it, and returns in a state of incapacity, surrendering to the doorsteps of majesty. How could a great Tablet be created from a tiny pearl? How could God have created the greatest thing from the smallest? The Tablet includes all times and all worlds: the physical, the spiritual, and the realm of invincibility (*mulk, malakūt, jabarūt*). Yet God created it from a pearl whose material body is smaller than that of the tablet. And though it is a registry (*dīwān*), if the human

---

160 This is a reference to the hadith that describes the Tablet as being created of pearls and rubies, which are created things.

being were to ponder it he would be unable to bring forth what is registered in it. This is the greatest proof of the deficiency of heedless intellects.

As for the knower of God, when he turns his intent to gaze at it, he pierces through the veils with his inner vision. In fact, if he turns his intent to anything at all, he pierces through it with his inner vision until God unveils for him the true nature of that thing. Thus, if you take two individuals, one of them a knower of God with inner vision and the other one veiled so that he sees nothing but the sensory realm, and they both look at a wall, for instance, the possessor of inner vision will pierce through it, while the other one will halt at the wall because he does not see anything else.

When something hidden behind the form of a thing is unveiled to the knower of God within his inner vision, it reflects upon his outward vision, and he witnesses what his inner vision saw with his outward vision. This is on account of the union of the light of outer vision with the Light of inner vision. Thus, when the knower of God has an unveiling with his inner vision and beholds unseen things, he sees with his outer vision the forms that he witnesses with the eye of his heart which are traced on the thing that he faces, engraved in space right in front of him. If he is facing a wall, he sees it in the wall; if his vision is turned toward his hand, he will see it in his hand, and so on. This is why the possessor of inner vision sees what veiled persons do not see. An example is what al-Bukhārī reported in *al-Tārīkh al-kabīr* on the authority of Anas ﷺ, who said: "I went out with the Prophet ﷺ to the mosque, where there were people raising their hand in supplication. He ﷺ said, 'Do you see in their hands what I see?' I said, 'What is in their hands?' He ﷺ said, 'In their hands is Light.' I said, 'Pray to God that He may show me the Light.' He ﷺ prayed to God, and He showed it to me. Then he ﷺ hurried, and we both raised our hands."[161] This hadith makes it clear that the one who possesses a piercing inner vision sees what those of a sensory realm do not see. And when the companion ﷺ asked the Prophet ﷺ to pray to God to let him see it, this showed that purity of inner vision is necessarily dependent upon an intermediary (*wāsiṭa*), and that is the presence of al-Muṣṭafā ﷺ. For the station of spiritual training (*tarbīya*) belongs to him ﷺ fundamentally, while to others—his heirs, the saints of his community—it belongs only through deputyship (*niyāba*).

You should also know, dear disciple, that whatever unveilings you receive are through the blessing of the supplication of your Shaykh, because your Shaykh is the one who intercedes for you so that the Light may enter into your heart. So do not presume that you attained it with your knowledge or your deeds. Sayyidunā Anas ﷺ knew this, which is why he asked for supplication from the Prophet ﷺ, so that the veils may be parted for him and he may experience this luminous witnessing. That is, he asked for the means of approach (*wāsila*) and the intermediary (*wāsiṭa*), then hurried to supplicate and draw near when he

---

161 Bukhārī, *al-Tārīkh al-kabīr*, 3:202; Bayhaqī, *Dalāʾil al-nubūwa*, 6:197.

saw the Light. Learn from him how to observe proper etiquette with the Light, and to greet it with surrender and humility to the Lord of Exaltedness, so that it may yield fruit in your heart.

Another hadith that clarifies what we are discussing is the hadith about the solar eclipse, narrated by Bukhārī and others. It tells of how the sun eclipsed for the first time in the Prophet's ﷺ lifetime after it had risen a bow's length above the horizon. The world grew dark, and people were alarmed. The Prophet ﷺ was so alarmed that he ﷺ rushed out to the mosque wearing only his waist-wrapper and leaving his cloak behind him. They went after him with his cloak, and he put it on and began to drag it behind him; that is, he did not stop to arrange it properly, so alarmed was he. He ﷺ ordered that the call be sounded for communal prayer, and all the people gathered together. The entire community, men and women, gathered with him, and the Prophet ﷺ led them in prayer, lengthening the standing, the bowing, and the prostration. As he prayed, the Garden and the Fire were displayed before him.

'Abdullāh b. 'Abbās said: "There was a sun eclipse and God's Messenger prayed, and the people prayed with him. He stood for a long time, nearly as long as [it takes to recite] Surah al-Baqara, and then he bowed for a long time. Then he rose and stood for a long time, though less than the first time. Then he bowed for a long time, though less than the first time. Then he went down into prostration. Then he stood for a long time, though less than the first time. Then he bowed for a long time, though less than the first time. Then he rose and stood for a long time, though less than the first time. Then he bowed for a long time, though less than the first time. Then he prostrated, and by the time he had finished the sun had reappeared. Then he said, 'The sun and the moon are two signs of God. They do not eclipse for anyone's death nor for anyone's life. When you see an eclipse, remember God.' They said, 'O Messenger of God, we saw you reaching out for something as you stood there, and then we saw you withdraw.' He said, 'I saw the Garden and reached out for a bunch of grapes from it. Had I taken it, you would have eaten from it for as long as this world lasts. And I saw the Fire. I have never seen anything like what I have seen this day, and I saw that most of its inhabitants were women.' They said, 'Why, O Messenger of God?' He said, 'Because of their ungratefulness (*kufr*).' Someone said, 'Are they ungrateful to God?' He said, 'They are ungrateful to their husbands and they are ungrateful to those who treat them virtuously. Even if you were to behave virtuously towards one of them for a whole lifetime and then she were to see you do something [that she did not like] she would say that she had never seen anything good from you.'"[162]

So the solar eclipse is one of the signs of God with which he strikes fear into his servants, as per the hadith. When the eclipse is at its peak, the vision of sensory things diminishes because of the difficulty of seeing in the dark. But by God's grace, this only lasts for a few minutes. As for the display of the forms of

---

162 Bukhārī, *Ṣaḥīḥ*, 5197.

the Garden and the Fire during the eclipse prayer, this was his ﷺ noble inner vision piercing through the wall as he stood facing it. He ﷺ turned with his inner vision to the abode of the hereafter, and saw it with his outer vision on full display upon a small corporeal body, namely the wall. God be glorified! How small is the size of the eye in which are imprinted the forms of the greatest corporeal bodies, such as the sky. And not only did the Lord bless the children of Adam with the ability to behold immense things with so small an eye, He also blessed them with inner vision by which they may see those things that lie beyond the sensory realm.

Another hadith which speaks of vision with the inner eye is related in Muslim's *Ṣaḥīḥ*, on the authority of ʿUthmān b. Abī al-ʿĀṣ, who came to the Prophet ﷺ and said, "Satan came between me and my prayer and caused confusion in my recitation." God's Messenger ﷺ said, "That is a devil named Khanzab. If you feel him coming, seek refuge in God and spit three times on your left side." The Companion later recalled, "I did so, and God banished him from me."[163]

Now in the imaginal sensory realm, Iblīs comes from four sides: front, behind, left, and right. He does not have the ability to come from above or below, because he has no control over the length of the *Alif*. This companion, may God be pleased with him, was attacked by Iblīs from the left side, because anything that is evil besets the wayfarers from the left side. In other

---

163 Muslim, *Ṣaḥīḥ*, 2:953.

words, whatever comes from the left side is lowly (*suflī*), and its energy is negative. And whatever is luminous, whether it be a jinn or an angel or the oaths of the Qur'ān, comes from the right side, which is why the Prophet ﷺ loved using his right in all affairs.

If the Garden and the earth both unveil themselves to the knower of God, for instance, he will see the Garden to his right and the earth to his left, because the Light and power of the Garden is stronger than that of the earth. For the eye has six muscles, and it sees in six directions. It is like a planet, turned by the muscles to the right, the left, above, and below. The little streaks in the iris within it contain a quantity of iron (*ḥadīd*). God says concerning vision, **You were indeed heedless of this, and now We have removed from you your cover, so today your sight is piercing** (also iron, *ḥadīd*).[164] Heedlessness is the cause of the weakening of vision. When the disciple increases his invocation, his vision becomes stronger and unites with his inner vision, so he attains piercing vision (*baṣar ḥadīdī*). *Ḥadīd*, iron, is the name of a Surah of the Qur'ān that begins with a verb in the past tense: *sabbaḥa* ("glorified," in the past tense), which is one of the expressions of praise of God, and it denotes continuity, meaning prior to vision, movement, and speech, such that just by virtue of inhaling and exhaling, the moment passes. The disciple must therefore increase his praise of God and his pondering of the heavens and the earth with invocation,

164 Q Qāf 50:22.

so that his vision may be sharpened by the metal of eternity.

Below is an illustration to help you understand the relationship between vision with the inner eye, when the heart is pure, and vision with the outer eye which only sees sensory objects:

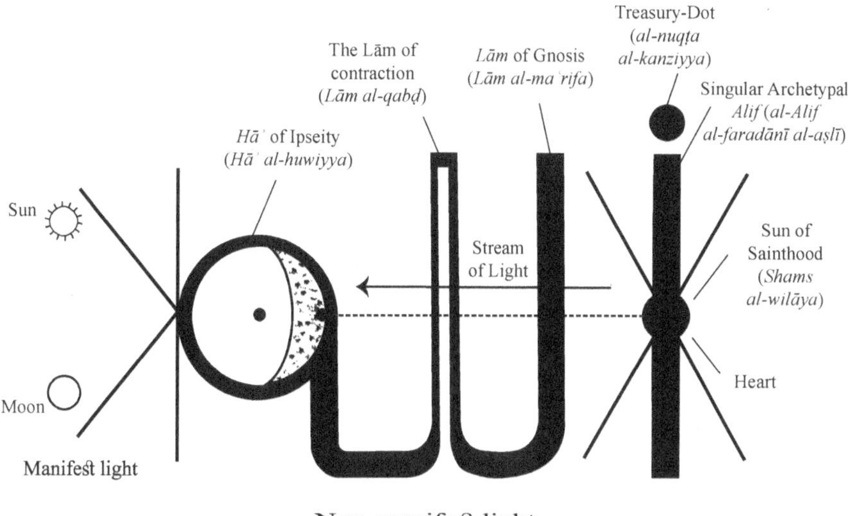

And here is a diagram of an eye that depends on outward Light, on the sun and the moon, for vision:

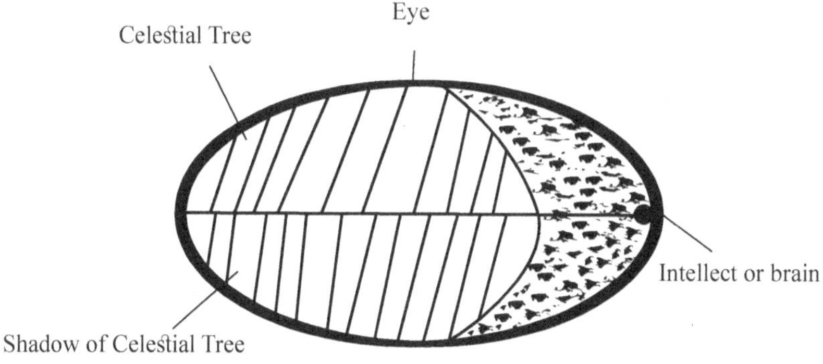

We have previously spoken about iron or piercing vision (*baṣar ḥadīdī*) which becomes virtually the same as inner vision because it is unified with it. A hadith tells of how the Prophet ﷺ said, "Verily, these hearts become rusted just as iron becomes rusty when it is exposed to water." He was asked, "O Messenger of God, how can they be polished?" He ﷺ replied, "By frequent remembrance of death, and the recitation of the Qur'ān."[165] Thus, God's Messenger ﷺ explained to us that the heart becomes rusty, and when it rusts, it veils the vision of the inner eye so that it only beholds the sensory realm, and the servant becomes veiled. But when he invokes God and connects his invocation to a continuous initiatic chain of Light, and the Light of the divinely-permitted invocation enters his heart, and bursts forth from the rock of his heart, and witnessings and divine disclosures are unveiled, they veil what the eye sees. The forms of sensory objects imprint themselves upon one's vision due to the Light of the sun and the moon, while direct witnessing springs forth from within, and delivers messages from the Light of the Hidden *Alif*, and the outer eye is exposed to them and it gives its news. Through this, the disciple comes to understand the messages of, **And He taught Adam the names, all of them.**[166]

From the hadith about the solar eclipse, we learn that the state of the disciple must be one of fear and alarm. He is assisted in this by remembering death, because that is what cuts off his

165 Bayhaqī, *Shuʿab al-Imān*, 3:392.
166 Q Baqara 2:31.

long term hopes and his love of the herebelow. The disciple must also prepare himself to be in a state that is generated by the solar eclipse, a state of darkness, especially at his beginning stage of wayfaring. He must close his eyes during the invocation, or devote for his soul one hour each night during the last third of the night, so that his luminosity grows stronger. He must not be distracted by the sensory faculties, and this is in order for other worlds to become unveiled for him, worlds that are not perceived by the sensory eye. For whatever forms of created things the eye sees, they imprint themselves upon the heart. So you must erase all of the forms from your heart with the Light of the Almighty in order for your vision to become piercing (*ḥadīd*), and in order for you to understand what Sayyidunā ʿAlī, may God ennoble his face, said concerning Sayyidunā ʿAbdullāh b. ʿAbbās ﷺ: "It is as if he beheld the unseen from behind a thin veil."

17.

I Become His Hearing
(*Kuntu Samʿahu*)

Mudhākara from the Friday
Gathering of 20th Jumādā al-Thāniya 1436/10th April 2015

Bismillāh al-Raḥmān al-Raḥīm

Know, dear wayfarer, may God reconnect your branch to your root, that during the last gathering we spoke about the station of vision with regard to the Holy Tradition, "I become the vision with which he sees." In this gathering, we will speak about the station of hearing with respect to the perfect servant (*al-ʿabd al-kāmil*) whose spiritual nature has mounted his bodily nature. So we say, with the grace of God, that hearing has three physical levels, as well as other divisions at the levels of the spiritual realm (*al-malakūt*) and the realm of invincibility (*al-jabarūt*).

The first level is to sense sound without understanding: you hear a sound, but do not comprehend its meaning. God says, **Deaf, dumb, and blind, they do not understand,**[167] likening the unbelievers to dumb beasts due to how they hear but do

---

167 Q Baqara 2:171.

not understand what they hear. When a shepherd is herding his flock and he commands them to go in a certain direction or to return in a certain direction, they do so even though they do not understand any of his words. Rather, they move out of habit. This level of hearing is common to the unbeliever and the beast.

The second level of auditory sense perception is to hear something and understand it. God says, **Do you hope then that they will believe you, seeing that a party of them would hear the word of God and then distort it after they had understood it, knowingly?**[168] Such people hear the rulings and understand them, but then change them. This verse was revealed with respect to the seventy men who were with Moses ﷺ, and how they changed and corrupted the commandments God had issued them.

The third level of auditory sense perception is to hear with understanding and to emulate. God says, **Only they are believers whose hearts quake with fear when God is mentioned, and when His signs are recited unto them, they increase them in faith, and they trust in their Lord.**[169] When they hear the word of God, their hearts are fearful and it increases them in faith. When they invoke God, they necessarily are fearful. Thus, they listen with presence of heart and ponder what they hear, and they trust in God because the Real has settled in their hearts, such that their hearts have become the throne of the

168 Q Baqara 2:75.
169 Q Anfāl 8:2.

name of God, *Allāh.* This is why trust in God (*tawakkul*) is the highest station of wayfaring, because it arises from the reality of divine unity.

The noble Qur'ān, furthermore, distinguishes between hearing (*samʿ*), listening (*istimāʿ*), inclining (*iṣghāʾ*), and listening attentively (*inṣāt*). It speaks of inadvertently hearing something without any intention on one's part, such as when you are in the market or a gathering and you hear false and idle chatter. Now you have a choice: to sit, or to turn away. God says, **And when they hear idle talk, they turn away therefrom and say, "Unto us our deeds, and unto you your deeds. Peace be upon you! We do not seek out the ignorant."**[170]

As for listening (*istimāʿ*), it is an intentional act because of one's immersion in hearing and discerning the meaning. God says, **And remember when we made a group of jinn incline to thee, listening to the Qur'ān.**[171] Saʿīd b. Jubayr ☙ said, "When the Prophet ﷺ was sent forth, the heavens were placed on guard and Satan said, 'These guards must have been set because something significant has happened on earth.' So he sent forth his troops through the earth, and they found the Prophet ﷺ standing in prayer at dawn with his companions by a palm tree, reciting. They listened until he had finished, and then **they went back to their people as warners. They said, "O our people! Truly we have heard a Book sent down after Moses, confirming that which came before it, guiding to the truth**

170 Q Qaṣaṣ 28:55
171 Q Aḥqāf 46:29.

and to a straight road.[172] This hadith is an evidence that listening (*istimāʿ*) occurs intentionally on the part of the listener.

As for inclining (*iṣghāʾ*), this is a level where concentration of hearing is combined with the reaction of the heart and emotions. God says, **If you both repent unto God, for your hearts did certainly incline.**[173] Thus, "inclining" is followed by none other than the application of what was said. If you listen indifferently without being moved to act, this means that your heart is veiled from what you hear; for if the Light of the speech entered your heart, your body would be stirred in service of it.

As for listening attentively (*inṣāt*), this is the highest level of hearing, the level that attracts divine mercy. God says, **And when the Qurʾān is recited, harken unto it and listen attentively that happily you may receive mercy.**[174] Thus, attentive listening is to listen along with the ability to read the meanings, wisdoms and secrets that lie beyond the words and letters. Such is the state with regard to the invoker: the circle of attentive listening must be made whole within him so that the divine mercies may descend upon him. This means to invoke with the tongue while understanding what one says, so that one's hearing receives it and it enters the heart, and so on, circling repeatedly between the tongue, the hearing, and the heart.

In more than one verse of His Holy Book, God mentions the faculty of hearing before the faculty of seeing, because it is the

172 Q Aḥqāf 46:29-30.
173 Q Taḥrīm 66:4.
174 Q Aʿrāf 7:204.

faculty that never stops working and never sleeps, in contrast to vision. God says, **So We placed a veil over their ears in the cave for a number of years.**[175] The meaning of this veiling is that God nullified their hearing and prevented them from hearing what was around them, so that they fell asleep for that long time that God had willed for them. This implies that the faculty of hearing usually does not sleep, which speaks to its greatness. God has instituted many norms for the circle of hearing. For instance, if sound rises above the capacity of the ear, the human being loses the faculty of hearing, and this affects the entirety of his body. God says, **It was but a single cry, then behold, they were extinguished.**[176] Thus, the hearing faculty is like an organ that fulfills its function in the herebelow. The fetus in the womb of the mother begins to hear the beats of its mother's heart in the fifth month, and when it is born, its hearing faculty is fully mature. This is why the Sunnah recommends giving the call to prayer (*ādhān*) and the *iqāma* in the ears of the newborn. As for the faculty of sight, it is only completed when the baby reaches seven months. As it were, the faculty of sight is only complete when the disciple completes the seven readings of the levels of the Name. When a human being is drugged or lacks oxygen, he loses the faculty of sight before hearing.

These virtues bring the circle of hearing to completion, such that it comprises three hundred and sixty complete degrees, meaning that the human being can hear from all directions,

175 Q Kahf 18:11.
176 Q Yāsīn 36:29.

in contrast to seeing, which he only takes from one hundred and forty-five or one hundred and eighty degrees, in the physical realm. However, in the spiritual realm, the circle of vision is also complete. Below is an illustration to bring this meaning closer to you:

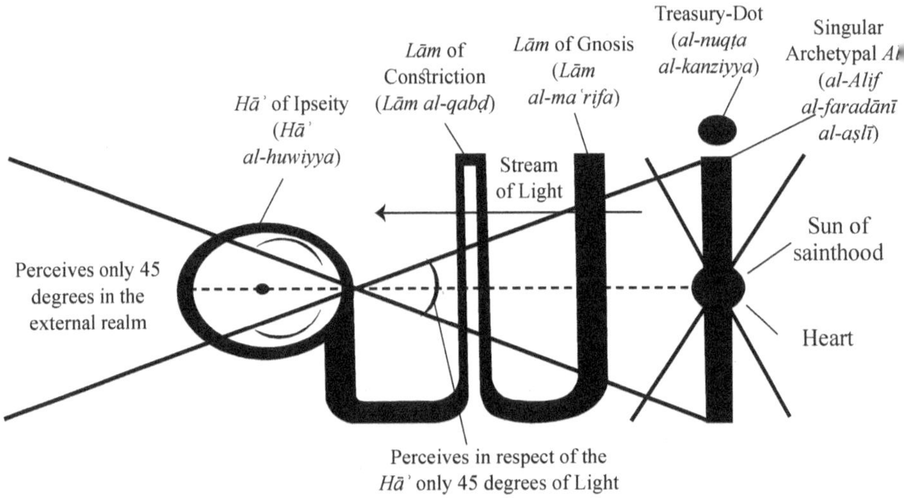

This illustration clarifies the difference between outward vision, which comes from the external realm in the form of light that is deciphered by the brain and grants you the ability to see one hundred and forty-five degrees from each angle, in contrast to inner vision *(baṣīra)*, where Light comes from within the *Hā'*, wherein is the Hidden *Alif*, and settles in your heart. For the innermost secret of the Name is read in the presence of the heart, and its beginning stage is seeing spiritual allusions. Then you enter into the *Hā'* and it gives you a widening that resembles the outward vision of the eye. This is why the disciple is able to count the directions in the spiritual realm even though there are only two directions therein. For even in the *Hā'*-center of the Hidden *Alif*, the *Lām Alif* (لا) is written for you like an X. As such, you learn annihilation (*fanā'*) through the *Lā* of negation by removing all things from your heart and witnessing the Real alone. Then when you see the Light, you bring it back from the spiritual realm to the physical realm, and from the center you come to see the Light from all directions.

Therefore, when you fare by virtue of the Light of **Guide us upon the straight Path**,[177] which is the line that was drawn by God's Messenger ﷺ in the sand, with respect to following the noble Law outwardly and inwardly, then you will only have two directions, because the illusory straight line divides the circle of *Hā'* into two halves. You see one hundred and eighty degrees from the higher side of the Tree, and one hundred and eighty degrees from the lower side[178] of the shade, and thus, the circle of your vision inwardly becomes complete, and the forms are negated for you by virtue of the rising of your spiritual aspiration above the here and the hereafter.

As for the circle of hearing, it is completed outwardly and inwardly at once, such that you hear from all directions. It possesses three hundred and sixty complete degrees. Below is an illustration which demonstrates the dot of hearing and its shape outwardly and inwardly.

---

177 Q Fātiḥa 1:6.
178 The Arabic text has "higher side" (*'ulwīya*), which is likely a misprint.

The outward physical hearing of the invoker and others is identical. This schematic diagram is also spiral-shaped, as per the shape of the eardrum. When vibrations from outside are detected by the eardrum, they reach the brain that decodes them.

Inner hearing in the shape of a spiral that perceives all the levels of the Name and covers the *Hā'*. When the wayfarer's luminous hearing unites with physical hearing by virtue of the invocation of the Singular Name, then he hears through God's hearing.

Thus, inner hearing becomes strengthened for the disciple when the Light of his heart is unified with the hearing faculty, in the sense of the hadith of the Beloved ﷺ who would supplicate on his way to the mosque, "Dear God, place Light in my heart, and Light in my hearing." When you attain this state by virtue of following and acting upon what you hear, your hearing radiates with the Light of "I become his hearing by which he hears," and you hear the disembodied voices (*hawātif*), innermost secrets, and glorifications of creatures. And all of this is by way of your outward ear, because the Light of your heart flows to your ear, so that when you hear it internally you are certain that it comes from your heart, because you hear it from a single direction. However, if you hear this disembodied voice from outside and you are certain of it but you are not sure where you heard it from, at that point you will have heard it from two directions. This is because the circle of your hearing widens until it attains to a high level, and that is by bringing the two upper levels down into the physical realm. Wherever you turn after that with the Light of your faith, you hear the glorification of creatures.

You should also know that the door of inner hearing will not open up for you until outwardly you begin to hear the words of your spiritual guide and follow them. As for the one who hears them and turns away, he has no share in this respect. This is well attested-to in the prophetic biography. It is related in the authenticated reports that Sayyidunā Abū Bakr, ʿUmar, and ʿUthmān, may God be pleased with them, all used to hear the glorifications of food in the Prophet's noble palm ﷺ. It is also transmitted in the authenticated reports that Sayyidunā ʿImrān b. Ḥusayn ؓ used to hear the greetings of peace of the angels. There are many similar instances in the books about the Prophet's life concerning the states of the companions, may God be pleased with all of them.

18.

I Become His Hand
(*Kuntu Yadahu*)

Mudhākara from the Friday
Gathering of 27th Jumādā al-Thāniya 1436/17th April 2015

Bismillāh al-Raḥmān al-Raḥīm

You should know, dear wayfarer, that we began to part the veils of the hadith of the saint, which expresses the lordly servant's realization of the saying "I become his hearing with which he hears, and his seeing with which he sees, and his hand with which he grasps, and his foot by which he walks." This hadith now invites us to delve into some of the hidden aspects of the physical hand. So we say, with God's grace:

The circle of the hand, from the shoulder to the ends of the fingertips, covers one hundred and eighty degrees, but from the side of the palm it only covers one hundred and forty-five degrees. Its attribute thus resembles that of the eye outwardly, but inwardly it is complete, and that is in the measure of the flow of God's Light through it. God says, **Those who pledge allegiance unto you pledge allegiance unto none other than God; the hand of God is above their hands.**[179] This refers to

---

179 Q Fatḥ 48:10.

the pledge of allegiance to the Chosen One ﷺ when the Muslims gave their allegiance to him, and the hand of the Real was all-encompassing. This is a verse of divine immanence (*tashbīh*), and can only be known through the *Kāf* of Immanence: 'As if you see Him' (*ka-annaka tarāhu*). This is why it is obligatory to believe in it just as it is, without explaining it away, while nevertheless believing in God's total transcendence. The way it is understood according to direct spiritual taste is that the hand of the Chosen One ﷺ was fully annihilated in the Real, and subsisted through the Real, and thus God was the One Who grasped with it and received the pledge of allegiance. This was without any indwelling, unification, or intermingling; for all these notions are forms of unbelief according to both the revealed Law and the esoteric reality.

Now, since he ﷺ was the complete and perfect manifestation-site of the holy realities, God says of him, **Whoever obeys the Messenger has obeyed God**,[180] thereby rendering obedience to him ﷺ as obedience to God. The circumstances behind the revelation of this verse was that the Prophet ﷺ used to say, "The one who obeys me has obeyed God, and the one who loves me loves God," and some hypocrites said, "This man just wants us to take him as a lord just as the Christians took ʿĪsā b. Maryam as their lord." Then the verse was revealed, confirming what he ﷺ had said.

---

180 Q Nisāʾ 4:80.

And since he ﷺ is the Seal of Prophets, he gave to his community a share of his inheritance when he said, "The scholars are the inheritors of the Prophets. The Prophets do not bequeath dinars or dirhams; they bequeath knowledge, and whoever takes it has inherited a great share."[181] Therefore, in each age, God manifests one of His saints to guide people back to their Lord and enable them to know Him, removing the covering of darkness from their hearts and renewing their religion for them. The revealed Law specifies that this occurs every hundred years. The Prophet ﷺ said, "God sends forth to this community, at the beginning of every hundred years, one who will renew for it its religion."[182] Through this reviver-saint, God revives the Light of faith in hearts, and through him the sun of spiritual excellence shines upon the spirit; yet God does not require that this saint be well known or famous, or that he have any followers. None of that is relevant, for what matters is that this renewer has realization of the station of sainthood, for it is therein that he is granted the banner of renewal. He is thus the locus of God's gaze. He is like the Kaʿba, which is the Kaʿba whether people circumambulate it or not, and whether people face it or not. The same goes for the prophets and messengers, whose specificity would remain immutable even if no one were to follow them. According to ʿAbdullāh b. ʿAbbās ﷺ, God's Messenger ﷺ said, "The communities were displayed before me, and I saw prophets with a few individuals, prophets with one

181 Tirmidhī, *Sunan*, 2:683.
182 Abū Dāwūd, *Sunan*, 2:753.

or two followers, and Prophets with no followers. Then I saw a great crowd, I thought that they were my nation, but I was told, 'That is Moses and his nation, but look to the horizon.' I looked and saw a massive gathering. Then I was told look to the other horizon, and there was another massive gathering. Then I was told, 'That is your nation. Among them are seventy-thousand who will enter the Garden without any accounting, and without any punishment.'"[183]

Now, the saint whose being comes to naught in the Lights of certainty becomes, in his true nature, the spirit of the religion and the true wellspring of the gardens of gnosis and certainty. For he is granted the secret of vicegerency in the footsteps of the Chosen One ﷺ. Indeed, he is his mirror, just as the mirror of Sayyidunā Muḥammad ﷺ is the form of the Real, as in the hadith of Abū Hurayra ؓ in which the Prophet ﷺ said, "God created Adam in His form."[184] The Messenger of God ﷺ also said, "The one who sees me has seen the Real."[185] This means whatever he ﷺ meant by it, without any suggestion of similarity, indwelling, or unification. Yet so long as tongues move in time and space and seek to express that which is hallowed beyond time and space, letters and words must necessarily involve similarity (*tashbīh*). But the one who wishes to be quenched from the gushing spring of prophetic gnosis must accompany his inheritors, who inherited from him some of his noble states.

183 Muslim, *Ṣaḥīḥ*, 1:112-113.
184 Bukhārī, *Ṣaḥīḥ*, 3:1267.
185 Muslim, *Ṣaḥīḥ*, 2:979.

This Muḥammadan inheritance disclosed itself especially in the household of God's Messenger 殺, in that many among the saints, past and present, appeared from among his offspring 殺.

'Abd al-Raḥmān b. Abī Laylā said, "Ka'b b. 'Ujra met me and said, 'Shall I not give you a gift?' Once the Prophet 殺 came out to us and we said, 'O Messenger of God, we know how to greet you, but how do we invoke blessings upon you?' He 殺 said, 'Dear God, bless Muḥammad and the family of Muḥammad as You blessed Ibrāhīm and the family of Ibrāhīm; truly You are Praiseworthy, Glorious. Dear God, send grace upon Muḥammad and the family of Muḥammad as You sent grace upon Ibrāhīm and the family of Ibrāhīm; truly You are Praiseworthy, Glorious.'"[186] Here the special status of the Prophet's Household is manifest, especially those who have realized the stations of sainthood and the Lights of the attributes and the all-comprehensive disclosure.

Jābir b. 'Abd Allāh said, "I saw God's Messenger 殺 during his Hajj on the Day of 'Arafa on his she-camel al-Qaṣwā' while he was preaching, and I heard him say, 'O mankind, I have left with you something that, if you take it, you will never go astray: the Book of God and my progeny, my Household.'"[187]

And at the stations of assuming character traits (*al-ittiṣāf*), the servant realizes the innermost secret of "I become his hand with which he grasps." This is because when the heart becomes filled with the Light of faith, it begins to flow sequentially from

186 Bukhārī, *Ṣaḥīḥ*, 3:1292.
187 Tirmidhī, *Sunan*, 2:962.

vision to hearing, then to the hand, and this becomes manifest for the people of inner vision. Anas b. Mālik said, "I went out with the Prophet ﷺ to the mosque, where there were people raising their hand in supplication. He ﷺ said, 'Do you see in their hands what I see?' I said, 'What is in their hands?' He ﷺ said, 'In their hands is Light.' I said, 'Pray to God that He may show me the Light.' He ﷺ prayed to God, and He showed it to me. Then he ﷺ hurried, and we both raised our hands."[188] Thus, when the Light reaches the hand, it gains a luminous power.

The revealed Law encourages the use of the hand when invoking God so that its luminosity may become strengthened. A hadith of Abū Hurayra ﷺ relates that he said, "I heard God's Messenger ﷺ say, 'The one who glorifies God after each prayer thirty-three times, and praises Him thirty-three times, and extols His greatness thirty-three times, making ninety nine, and then says at the hundredth, "There is no god but God, alone without partner; His is the kingdom, and His is the praise, and He has power over all things" (*Lā ilāha illā Allāh waḥdahu lā sharīka lahu, lahu al-mulk wa-lahu al-ḥamd wa-huwa ʿalā kulli shayʾin qadīr*), his sins will be forgiven even if they be like the foam of the ocean.'"[189] Another hadith of Yasīra ﷺ, one of the Migrants (*muhājirāt*), relates: "God's Messenger ﷺ said, 'I encourage you to invoke glorification of God (*tasbīḥ*, i.e. *subḥān Allāh*), oneness of God (*tahlīl*, i.e. *lā ilāha illā Allāh*), holiness

---

188 Bayhaqī, *Dalāʾil al-nubūwa*, 6:197.
189 Muslim, *Ṣaḥīḥ*, 1:238.

of God (*taqdīs*), and count using your fingers, because they will be asked and given the power to speak. Do not be heedless, lest you forget God's mercy.'"[190]

These two hadiths illustrate the virtue of glorification, since these invocations are associated with virtue and the erasure of sins though they be as numerous as foam of the ocean. The Prophet ﷺ established a link between glorification, extolling God's greatness, and praise (*tasbīḥ*, *takbīr*, and *taḥmīd*), and the ebb and flow of the ocean, because that is the cause of the generation of foam. It is the moon that affects this process, and the secret of this is that when a human being moves his fingers, it is as if he is moving the celestial body of the moon through all of its mansions. There are fourteen divisions in the right hand and fourteen in the left, which alludes to the total number of the mansions of the moon. This is also the number of the luminous letters which comprise the oaths of the Qur'ān (*al-qawāsim*) and the Light's shadow. Thus, it is as if when one of the hands is in a state of glorification, that hand is in a luminous state, whereas the other hand is in the Light's shadow.

Hence, the emphasis on fasting on the white days (*al-ayyām al-bīḍ*): the thirteenth, fourteenth, and fifteenth of the lunar month when the moon is full and shining. Fasting on these days is equivalent to having fasted the entire year, because you transfer from a state of separation to union, or from the shadow of Light to Light. It is specifically during this period that a person's

---

190 Tirmidhī, *Jāmiʿ*, 2:918.

appetites increase, because they are in a state of total separation. The three days are a manifestation-site for the lower triangle (*al-muthallath al-suflī*), which is why most sins are committed during these days. Thus, the revealed Law encourages bridging its separation by the fast or the remembrance of God.

We say also in this manner that as you glorify, it is as if you are moving the moon through its mansions and therefore your ebb and flow gains an equilibrium if you glorify after each prayer, but if you forget to do so then you will lose your equilibrium.

The human body contains a high percentage of water, around seventy or seventy-one percent, which is equal to the proportion of water on planet earth. It is as if the earth is a great man and you are a small earth—within you are rivers, valleys, oceans, freshwater and saltwater like the water of the ocean, which kills the bacteria and germs that enter your body. And just as the moon revolves around the earth and the earth around the sun, which gives life, you also contain the same movement within you.

So if you return to the luminous hand by which you glorify, then your flow will become natural, and your body will gain equilibrium, and your water will become pure and fresh. And when you fast during the middle of the month, you will gain dominance over your lower self, and you will deal death to disobedience, and your hand will become a full sky, not just the fingers.

God says, **We will show them our signs on the horizons and in themselves until it becomes clear to them that it is the**

truth.[191] So when you look within yourself with your piercing vision, you will find that every organ within you has a relationship to the cosmos in respect of union and separation. For instance, the hand represents the solar system, and at the same time it represents a dot in a particular mansion of the moon. The tip of the thumb has a connection to the brain, and when administering proper Islamic talismanic healing (*ruqya al-sharʿiya*), when you recite the Qur'ān over a person while holding on to the tip of his thumb and he begins to cry out, you should know that the demonic counterpart (*qarīn*) has taken up residence in his brain. But if you place your hand at the end of the thumb while reciting and the patient cries out, you should know that the demonic counterpart dwells in the nerves. As for the index and middle fingers, they both have a connection to the demonic breath (*al-ṭārīq*). If the patient feels pain at the lower part of these fingers, then his illness stems from the evil eye. As for the ring and pinkie fingers, at the upper part it is an expression of the higher energy (*al-ṭāqa al-ʿulwīya*), and if the person is engaging with the lower axis of himself from a place of psychic desire, in order to gain contact with jinn and to use them as servants, then this causes a negative result and a lower power which causes illness. As for the lower part of the two smaller fingers, it has a connection to the demonic counterpart's whisperings (*waswās*) in the hearing, which manifests during prayer. Moreover, the heart is located beneath the pinkie

191 Q Fuṣṣilat 41:53.

finger, which is why the count of the glorification of the *bāqiyāt al-ṣāliḥāt* begins with the lower part of the pinkie. When you take the thumb and place it on the point of the pinkie corresponding to the heart, you are moving the upper sphere within you, which brings together the heart and the intellect.

At the level of the celestial bodies, the thumb represents Venus (*al-Zuhra*); the index finger represents Jupiter (*al-Mushtarī*); and the middle finger represents Saturn (*Zaḥil*), and its color is black. This is why the Masonic symbols use this middle finger. As for the ring finger, it represents the Moon, Mars (*al-Mirrīkh*), and Mercury (*'Uṭārid*), and thus it represents the entire family. This is why al-Muṣṭafā ﷺ used to place his ring on it. As for the pinkie, it represents the Sun. The sites of all these corresponding locations are at the bottoms of the fingers. You should also know that we mentioned only some of these inner illnesses which exist in the hand, and we only mentioned some of the celestial spheres associated with it. There remain many properties and inner secrets which are brought together by God in the hand of the child of Adam.

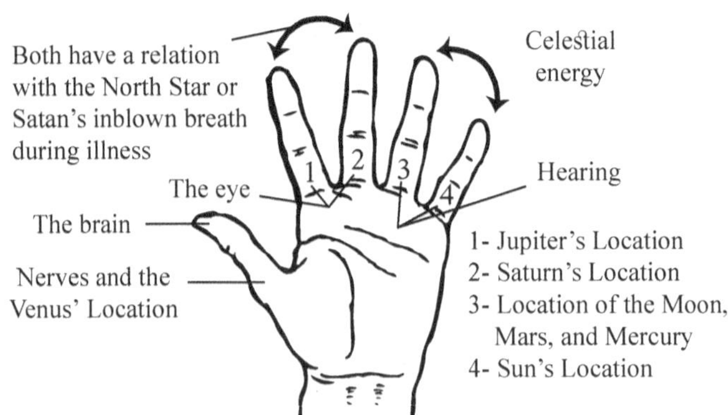

The hand resembles the written form of the divine name. The Hidden *Alif* is the pinkie where the dot below it is. The next finger is the *Lām* of Gnosis, which is why the ring, the seal of sainthood, was placed upon it. It is followed by the *Lām* of Constriction because that is the longest finger and it has a claim to selfishness. Then the index finger and the thumb are like the open *Hā'* at the end.

The right hand contains eighteen divine names, and the left hand eighty-one. The sum total of that is brought together in the all-encompassing name *Allāh*. When you kiss the hands of your fellow *fuqarā'*, you kiss the divine name. This is why kissing the hand is obligatory in our Path. This is also why the hand will bear witness against you on the Day of Resurrection, as if the stations of the moon and the luminous letters are bearing witness against you. The deeds that you perform are registered in your fingers. So do not touch anything with your hand other than the good, may God have mercy on you, so that the lunar luminous stations may testify for you. The more the hand is filled with Light, the more one completes its three hundred and sixty degrees, and one begins to radiate with the secret of "I am the hand with which he grasps." Similarly, the hand of Moses ﷺ was white for all to see; its Light more radiant than the sun. Moreover, those who pledge allegiance to the saint see the Lights flowing from his hand to theirs. God says, **And he pulled out his hand, and it was white for all to behold.**[192]

___

192 Q A'rāf 7:108.

19.

I Become His Foot
(*Kuntu Qadamahu*)

Mudhākara from the Friday
Gathering of 5th Rajab 1436/24th April 2015

Bismillāh al-Raḥmān al-Raḥīm

Know, may God aid you with His assistance, that with respect to the everlasting presence, the special Light that is deposited in the foot at the station of sainthood as described in the well-known Holy Tradition is the Light of stability and fixity. God bestows this Light upon the one who truly realizes divine assistance for and through God. God says, **O you who believe, if you assist God, He will assist you and make firm your feet.**[193] So making the feet firm comes after divine assistance, which is why the foot is mentioned among the last stations of being, because it is a sign of the Light's full flow throughout the entire body.

God makes the feet firm only after assisting a person in overcoming their lower self for a wise reason. For prior to God's assistance in overcoming a trial, a sickness, or a tribu-

193 Q Muḥammad 47:7.

lation, many to turn to God outwardly and seem to cling to the door of the Lord. But few remain firm in their victory after the blessing. For during times of ease, financial comfort, and health, the lower self forgets the blessing and tends to disobey God. None remain firm in obedience and good deeds after receiving God's gifts, except those who are **true to that which they pledged unto God.**[194]

Thus, you find that the disciple, before his spiritual opening and before the retreat (*khalwa*), exerts a lot of effort and is very active, but after his spiritual opening and after coming out of the retreat, his effort is transformed into laziness, his activity into weakness. This is because he halts at the gift and forgets the Giver, which is a great fracture in the lower self. The foot is therefore specific to you, O disciple, so will you have a firm footing or will you slip?

God says, **if you assist God, He will assist you and make firm your feet.**[195] This is both a threat and a motivation for the people of admonition and the people of reminder who call upon their Lord; those who seek to assist God's religion and to guide God's servants to love and obey God. So ask yourself, do you truly call unto God, or does your envy prevent you from loving good for others? Abū Dardā' said, "If you wanted, I could swear to you that the most beloved servants unto God are those who love God and make God's creatures love God. And if you wanted, I could swear to you that the most beloved servants of

194 Q Anfāl 33:23.
195 Q Muḥammad 47:7.

God are the caretakers of the sun and the moon, who walk upon the earth offering good counsel."[196] The Prophet ﷺ said, "People are God's dependents (*'iyāl Allāh*). The most beloved unto Him are those who benefit His dependents the most."[197] The greatest benefit is to guide to God, because it is the cause of everlasting felicity.

What it means for the servant to assist God is for him to struggle against his lower self, his caprice, and his devil, because they are God's enemies. When he is sincere in that, God gives him strength and helps him against them by repelling their evil from him and by placing him upon the straight Path of obedience to God. And He rewards him by unveiling His beauty so that he may stand firm at the station of servanthood. The Shaykh brings all this goodness together for you, because when he gives you the Light and asks you to assist him over the darkness which is within you, he wants you to assist God against the idol of your own ego. This is why sometimes he manifests the Light for you, and sometimes he hides it from you, in order to wake you up, so that you may remain on the straight Path and become alert. So listen actively to everything that your spiritual guide tells you, so that your Light will not be extinguished entirely. We seek refuge in God from being deprived after having been given!

A sound heart is either a star or a moon. Therefore, in order for your feet to stand firm, you must first struggle at the level of

---

196 Ibn al-Jarrāḥ, *Kitāb al-zuhd*, 339.
197 Ibn al-Tamīmī, *Musnad Abū Yaʿlā al-Mawṣilī*, 6:65.

the eyes, the ears, and the hands, so that you may arrive at the specific quality of "I become the leg by which he walks," because the Light moves from your heart to your limbs until it arrives at your foot. The Light of the foot is connected to the Light of the heart, and the Light of the heart to the Light of the spirit, and the Light of the spirit to the Light of the Secret (*nūr al-sirr*). It is thus that assistance upon God's Path discloses itself to you the physical realm. So observe your foot, where it takes you, and what type of companion is it? For inviting others to the Path requires sure-footedness, which is constancy until the Day of Resurrection.

Verse: **He said, "What was your purpose O Samaritan?" He said, "I saw that which they saw not, so I took a handful of dust from the footsteps of the Messenger, and I cast it. Thus did my soul prompt me."**[198] This means that the foot leaves a trace, and the trace has power and energy. Consider the hoof-print of the horse of Gabriel ﷾, how it instilled life into inanimate things. How therefore would you not be revived by kissing the footsteps of the knowers of God, or by kissing their feet with your heart? In fact, all those who surrender to them and kiss their feet are revived in spirit. Their Lights radiate, and they attain realized knowledge of God; for surrendering to the saints is surrendering to God, and the door of pre-eternity (*qidam*) is at their feet (*aqdām*). So prostrate before them, and the doors will open to you.

198 Q Ṭāhā 20: 95-96.

Moreover, since the foot's firmness becomes manifest by inviting others to the Path, the Prophet ﷺ said, "Convey on my behalf, even if it be a single verse."[199] Here he is specifically addressing those whose hearts are radiant with Light. In contrast, darkness it only guides unto darkness. So convey the Message once you become a niche of Light.

Additionally, since the principle of union (*jam'*) and separation (*farq*) governs every particle in existence, the foot of the child of Adam follows this pattern as well. For it is a union from one respect and a separation from another. It is a union because it brings together within its fold everything that the human being contains, and it is a separation in the sense that it is a part of the human body. In order to understand this better, contemplate this illustration which shows how some parts of the body reside in the foot.

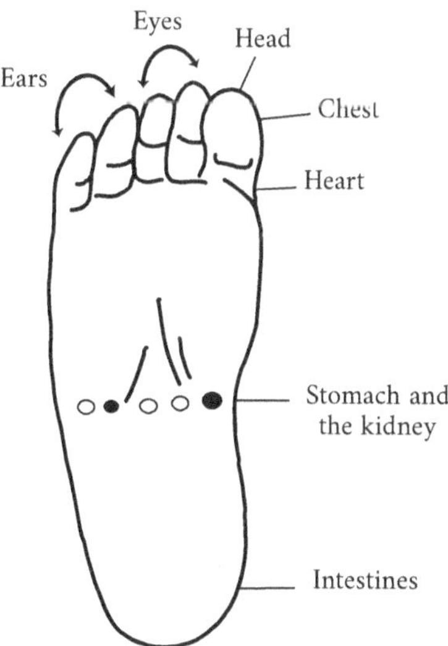

199 Bukhārī, *Ṣaḥīḥ*, 2:683.

With regard to the inner ailments of the spirit which beset the human being, including evil eye, magic spells, or obsessive whispering (*waswasa*), they too are centered in their places at specific points on the foot, such that you can identify the type of ailments just by studying those points. Here is an example of some of the ailments and their places in the foot.

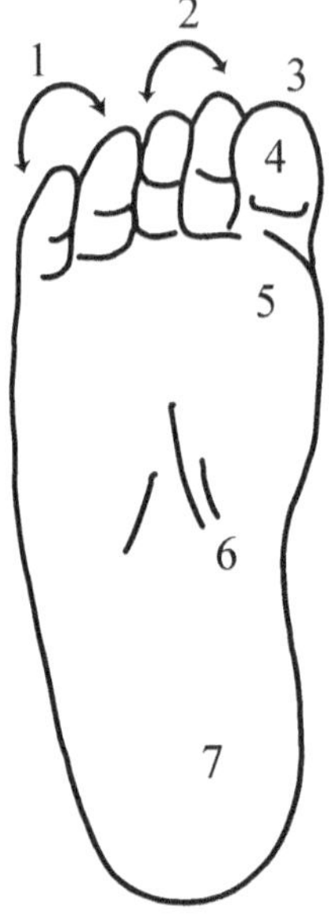

1. Demonic whispers
2. Evil eye
3. Lack of air
4. Air magic
5. Fire magic that requires incense to be smelled
6. Water magic (applied by spraying water) that requires an amulet (ruqya) using water
7. Buried earth magic that must be unearthed.

If the human being is suffering from an ailment of the spirit, and you grasp his big toe while reciting the noble Qur'ān and he begins to cry out, then you should know that his demonic counterpart (*qarīn*) is affecting him at the level of the head. In this manner, you can grasp any part of the foot while reading God's Word, and if he cries out you know that he is afflicted as we have shown in the illustration above.

The cure must be of the same type as the ailment, meaning that if the magic uses water then the healing through the recitation of the Qur'ān must be done over water, with which he can then wash himself and drink. If the magic is of the earth, that is, if it is buried under the earth, the treatment is to dig it up and nullify it, and so on. Now the evil eye, the touch (*mass*), and magic are real, and it is not permissible to deny this.

Bukhārī and Muslim narrate that 'Ā'isha told of how God's Messenger ﷺ was affected by a spell, and began to imagine that he had done things which in fact he had not done. She said, "One day when he ﷺ was with me, he invoked God for a long time and then said, 'O 'Ā'isha, do you know that God has instructed me regarding the matter I asked Him about? Two men came to me, and one of them sat by my head, the other by my feet. One said to the other, 'What is this man's ailment?' The other replied, 'He is under the effect of magic.' The first one asked, 'Who has worked magic on him?' The other replied, 'Labīd b. A'ṣam.' The first asked, 'By what means?' The other replied, 'With a comb and hair stuck to it, and the spathe of a spadix of a male date palm.' The first asked, 'Where is it?' The other replied, 'In the well of Dharwān.' Then the Prophet ﷺ went along with some of his Companions to that well. Then he returned to me and said, 'By God, the water of that well was red like the infusion of henna leaves, and its date palms were like the heads of devils.' I asked, 'O Messenger of God, did you take it out?' He replied, 'No, for God has healed me, and I was afraid that by showing it to the people I would spread evil among them.' Then he ordered that the well be filled with earth, and it was."[200]

In summary, when the Light flows to the foot it obliterates all darkness, and through it the servant acquires firmness and stability. In order for you to know the elevated status of the foot, ponder how God placed it as a sign that stands to our day in the Kaʿba where the Station of Abraham ﷺ is located. The trace of his noble foot is still etched there. Ibn ʿAbbās ﷺ narrates that when Abraham ﷺ was building the House, Ishmael handed him the rocks. Then when the Kaʿba grew taller, he had to stand on a rock, and his foot left a print on it. That is the Station of Abraham ﷺ. The remaining noble footprint of the prophet is a sign of the luminous force of Abraham's foot ﷺ. So if we say that the foot brings together the entirety of the possessor of that foot, this means that Abraham ﷺ exists therein. According to Jābir ﷺ, when the Prophet ﷺ finished his circumambulation of the Kaʿba, he prayed two cycles of prayer at the Station, then recited, **Take the station of Abraham as a place of prayer. And we made a covenant with Abraham and Ishmael: "Purify my house for those who circumambulate, those who make retreat, and those who bow and prostrate."**[201] The station is taken by the knowers of God as a *qibla* for their hearts, who purified it from all that is other-than-God. Whoever attains it is safe from the obsessive whisperings of the devil. For the people of the elect (*ahl al-khuṣūṣīya*), the inner Station of Abraham ﷺ

---

200 Ibid., 3:1192.
201 Q Baqara 2:125.

is immersion in the very entity of direct witnessing such that the Light takes charge over every particle of your body, and you come to naught in it at the level of the foot. This is why the wayfarer does not stand upon a foot of Light until he calls to God alone without partner.

20.

Adam's Image
(*Ṣūrat Adam* ﷺ)

Mudhākara from the Friday
Gathering of 12th Rajab 1436/1st May 2015

Bismillāh al-Raḥmān al-Raḥīm

Abū Hurayra ﷺ related that the Prophet ﷺ said, "God created Adam in His image, sixty cubits tall.[202] When He created him, He said, 'Go and greet that group of angels sitting there, and heed what reply they give you, for that will be your greeting and the greeting of your offspring.' Adam ﷺ went and said, '*al-salām 'alaykum*,' and they replied '*al-salām 'alayka wa-raḥmat Allāh*,' adding '*wa raḥmat Allāh*.' So whoever enters Paradise will be in the image of Adam, and the physique of human beings continues to decrease down to the present day."[203]

Thus, those who enter the garden, that is the garden of Gnostic sciences (*jannat al-ma'ārif*) or the garden of ornaments (*zakhārif*), enter in the image of Adam ﷺ. If you are a possessor of esoteric realities, and if you understand pure meaning, then approach this hadith with respect to the two halves in the

202 Approximately fifteen meters.
203 Bukhārī, *Ṣaḥīḥ*, 3:1267-1268.

manner of the *Lām* of Constriction (*lām al-qabḍ*), for we are about to enter through the *Lām*-reading itself. Thus, this hadith is divided into two: a half in which you have no share because it is sheer lordship; and a half in which you have a share, which is sheer servanthood.

If you want to attain the gardens, you must return to your original form. And since that which is with God can only be attained through God, the formula *wa-raḥmat Allāh* was added to the greeting by the angels, so that you may know that mercy is what enables you to attain genuine gnosis, so that you may take on the Adamic image. Muslim relates on the authority of Abū Hurayra ﷺ that God's Messenger ﷺ said, "If one of you fights his brother, he should avoid striking him in the face, for God created Adam in His image."[204] God's Messenger ﷺ also said, "Do not ask God to deform faces, for the children of Adam were created in the image of the All-Merciful (*'alā ṣurat al-Raḥmān*)."[205] The meaning of image (*ṣūra*) here is that which corresponds to the all-encompassing divine name *Allāh*. And in order for you to know that this specificity in the created nature of Adam ﷺ is not restricted to him alone, the aforementioned hadith prohibits striking the face or deforming it, thereby showing us that the transfer of the image continues through all of Adam's offspring after him.

This divine image is the one upon which God created the Perfect Man (*al-insān al-kāmil*). It is an all-encompassing presence

204 Muslim, *Ṣaḥīḥ*, 2:1108.
205 Ibn Abī ʿĀṣim, *Sunna*, 362.

for all the name-presences scattered throughout the cosmos. This all-comprehensive inclusiveness is what is expressed by the term vicegerency (*khilāfa*), which is singled out by knowledge of the most beautiful names of God. Thus God says, **And He taught Adam all the names.**[206] It was this vicegerency that distinguished Adam above the angels, such that they prostrated before him. Their prostration was toward his centrality (*markazīya*), and he was their *qibla* before the manifestation of Mecca and the Inhabited House (*al-bayt al-maʿmūr*).[207] For God created him in His image, and his image is none other than his innate disposition (*fitra*), which is none other than the pure realities of His essence. Therefore, if we understand what it means to be created upon the innate disposition of submission (*fiṭrat al-islām*), then we will understand the meaning of *al-salām ʿalayka*, "peace be upon you." And at that point, God's mercy will be unveiled to us, which comprises the presences of that Essence. Ruling authority (*ḥukm*) therefore belongs to this all-comprehensive totality which is described as the level of divinity (*martabat al-ulūhīya*). It is this totality that possesses all of the most beautiful names, and we are commanded to proclaim its oneness so that the matter may become clear to us from within ourselves.

Therefore, should anyone wish to part the veils of the talisman of his own soul, as God alerts us in the verse, **And within**

---

206 Q Baqara 2:31.
207 *Al-Bayt al-maʿmūr* is the celestial prototype of the earthly Kaʿba.

your souls, do you not then behold?[208] which we explained as the reflection of the Light upon your worlds—the one who yearns to attain direct knowledge of the gate of the divine name must search for the one whose image is in direct accordance with Adam's image ﷺ, because the soul can only be understood through the secret of God's words, **O mankind reverence your Lord who created you from a single soul, and from it created its mate, and from the two has spread abroad a multitude of men and women. Reverence God, through whom you demand your rights of one another, and family relations. Truly, God is a watcher over you.**[209] This servant-master is the **single soul** (*al-nafs al-wāḥida*) by virtue of the all-comprehensiveness from which all the particular souls gushed forth after He manifested from it its mate (*zawj*), which is his very own self since it came forth from him, so that there is no alterity.

The Eve of the soul (*Ḥawwā' al-nafs*) is one of the levels of the Adam of the spirit (*Adam al-rūḥ*), and the purpose behind this was the attainment of a multitude from that soul despite its being one. When you come to naught and reunite the branch with the root, you will understand my words. So guard your soul by first beholding its all-comprehensiveness, and do not be heedless with respect to it lest Iblīs confuse you. When you encounter the possessor of the all-comprehensive soul (*ṣāḥib al-nafs al-kullīya*), he will bring you out from the darkness to directly witness the Lights of lordship.

208 Q Dhāriyāt 51:21.
209 Q Nisā' 4:1.

The difference between the first mention of reverence: **O mankind. reverence your Lord,** and the second one: **And reverence God, through whom you demand your rights of one another, and family relations,** is that the first descends during the stage of servanthood while the second is a return from darkness to the Lights of lordship upon the realization of union. This is in order for the servant to learn constant self-examination (*murāqaba*), along with complete witnessing. Or, in order for him to learn annihilation and subsistence so that in his prayer he reaches the description of the Prophet ﷺ, "Grant us repose through the prayer, O Bilāl" (*ariḥnā bi-hā yā Bilāl*). Repose does not settle in the house of the heart until the breast is expanded with the Lights, whereupon the servant discovers the sweetness of worship and the repose of mastership (*siyāda*). However, if he finds heaviness in the prayer, he should know that he is in a state of distance from God.

So are you in the image of Adam, or in the image of Iblīs who flows through the blood of Adam?

God says, **O you who believe, reverence God, and let every soul consider what it has sent forth for tomorrow. And reverence God. Truly God is aware of whatever you do. And be not like those who forget God such that He makes them forget their souls. It is they who are iniquitous.**[210] The tongue of direct witnessing yields that the verse, **O you who believe, reverence God,** means to do so while witnessing something

---

210 Q Ḥashr 59:18-19.

alongside God, and this is by directing your reverence towards that all-comprehensive soul, the one which, when one witnesses it directly, one witnesses its Existentiator (*Mūjid*). Then the verse continues: **and let every soul consider what it has sent forth for tomorrow,** that is, by way of gnosis, because direct witnessing on the Day of Resurrection is in the measure of gnosis in the herebelow, for the herebelow is the counterpart of the hereafter, and there are many hadiths which clarify this, even with regard to the state of entry of some people of Paradise into Paradise. If someone is ignorant of God in this world, his ignorance will not be lifted with his death. Yes, the world of the hereafter will be unveiled to him, as will his station, but he will not have direct knowledge of his Lord because he did not have it in the herebelow. Then the verse repeats: **And reverence God** again; that is, do not seek anyone other than Him, because everything apart from God is illusion and imagination. Then the verse continues: **be not like those who forget God;** that is, those who forget to invoke Him, to turn to Him, and to expose themselves to His Lights, **such that He makes them forget their souls;** that is, He makes them indifferent to rectifying and healing their own souls, until they die in the valleys of incoming thoughts and doubts, deprived of self-knowledge. **It is they who are iniquitous,** outside of the Holy Presence. The verse continues: **Not equal are the inhabitants of the Fire and the inhabitants of the Garden;**[211] that is, the fire of deprivation and veil-

---

211 Q Ḥashr 59:20.

ing, and the garden of gnosis and arrival. **The inhabitants of the Garden are the triumphant**; they attain their Beloved and are delivered from every veil.

So turn to your soul and rectify it, so long as your appointed hour is still ahead of you, in the hopes that you too may have a portion from the Light of al-Muṣṭafā ﷺ, or lest you be expelled from the All-Holy Presence. The disciple is the one who lives for his future, while the heedless one lives with his past. If you wish to be among those who are intelligent, ask yourself, "What have I prepared for it by way of provision?" Ask yourself and think deliberately: are you one of the people of the past which has passed away, or do you look forward to divine proximity? Are you one of those who use their past as a mount toward the absolute? Do not stop with things other-than-God, while the door is open before you with all of its Lights. Remember that the hypocrite and the believer both gaze at the cosmos, but the believer looks at what is beyond it. All of them look at the physical constructs (*mabānī*), but only the believer sees the constructs and the pure meanings that lie beyond them. He beholds the veils (*astār*) as well as the Lights (*anwār*) beyond them. So search for your Adamic image in order to truly know God.

21.

He Who Knows Himself Knows His Lord
(*Man ʿArafa Nafsahu ʿArafa Rabbahu*)

Mudhākara from the Friday
Gathering of Rajab 19th 1436/8th May 2015

Bismillāh al-Raḥmān al-Raḥīm

God says, **Inner visions have come to you from your Lord, so whoever sees clearly, it is to the benefit of his own soul; and whoever is blind, it is to his detriment. I am not a keeper over you.**[212] Inner visions (*baṣāʾir*, sing. *baṣīra*) outwardly are demonstrations, proofs, and clarities that result from careful discernment. Inwardly, however, they are the visions that penetrate and pierce through the veils of the intellect. Inner vision sees pure meanings (*maʿānī*), while outer vision sees receptacles (*awānī*). Inner vision is opened by God for those of His servants whom He loves, and its sign is the shining of the Lights in the witnessing of the heart, until it covers the entire body in all directions. Then the boundaries and delimitations vanish from him, and he becomes a pure servant of God. Whoever

---

212 Q Anʿām 6:104.

223

sees this clearly is upon manifest guidance with his own self; and whoever is blind to it, it is to his own detriment.

The servant's first foot upon the Path is receiving inner visions and clearing away the darkness of existent things from his heart. This is when the flashes (sing. *bāriqa*) and the gleams (sing. *lāmiʿa*) become manifest for him for a single glimmer (*lamḥa*), until he becomes firmly fixed in witnessing them. This first ray of inner vision enables you to witness the proximity of the Real to you. The disciple must observe proper courtesy during the state of their manifestation to him, because in that moment he is the presence of the Generous. Then, the servant ascends to the eye of inner vision (*ʿayn al-baṣīra*), which enables him to witness his own non-existence and the existence of God, the Real. The direct tasting of this is when your body of darkness passes away for you, and you subsist by the lordly Light. Then, the servant ascends from this witnessing-site to witnessing the reality of inner vision (*ḥaqq al-baṣīra*), where he comes to know the meaning of neither non-existence nor existence. This is the spring source where the opposites unite and union and separation are directly known, and where the reality of "God was, and there was nothing with Him" is directly discovered. If he is able to drink from this overflowing ocean, then he stands at the podium of the eye of inner vision, which is the station where he directly witnesses the existence of the Real in the presence of neither non-existence nor existence.

Then, the knower of God sees nothing in the mirror of his

heart except for the Real. He has one side turned towards lordship by way of his non-delimited spirituality, through the properties of divine power, and another towards his own human nature, which is delimited by the properties of divine wisdom, and which subsists through the secret of divine sustenance (*qayyūmīya*). At this witnessing-site, proximity and distance come to naught, because the two mirrors, the spiritual and the human, both belong to the liminal self (*al-nafs al-barzakhīya*) which brings together the manifest arc (*al-qaws al-ẓāhirī*) and the non-manifest arc (*al-qaws al-bāṭinī*). This is only the case for the knower of God who has achieved mastery (*tamakkun*) and not for the beginner.

God says, **He will recompense them for their own character. Truly He is Wise, Knowing.**[213] Thus, God recompenses His servant in a manner that is commensurate with his own character. If a person honors the other, God honors him; if he belittles the other, God belittles him; if he is virtuous toward the other, God is virtuous toward him; and if he harms the other, He will be recompensed by his own character. Those who are characterized by separation will be separated by God; those who are characterized by union will be united by God, and so on. You drink the water you drew. When the esoteric realities become unveiled, you will know what your pen has written down in your own book. So use a luminous and elevated ink, and avoid lowly and dark ink. Inscribe upon the tablet of your soul what-

---

213 Q Anʿām 6:139.

ever you wish, with whatever ink you wish, for the sword of the verse, **And We did not wrong them, but they wronged themselves**[214] rules over you. You are the one who wrongs yourself by your own self if you ignore the reality of yourself. The one who sees his own character is never wronged. You rule over yourself, through yourself, for yourself, in the mirror of your essence. Thus, the ruling properties of your own image all return back upon you. You are today building castles in the Garden or digging pits in the Fire, and no one has wronged you.

The secret behind this matter is that you are the vicegerent as well as the purpose behind creation. If only you were to open the eye of your heart to the book of your soul, and to read the pure meaning of the verse, **And in your, souls do you not see?**[215] and if only you were to attain the key to the treasure of "He who recognizes himself recognizes his Lord." The soul is the mirror for the genuine character traits, and no one can have knowledge of their soul unless they lower themselves before one who can teach them how to return back to the primordial inblowing (*nafkha al-aṣlīya*), and who can erase the shadow of their own existence from the mirror of their heart. Only then are the Lights disclosed, and only then is one's foot firmly rooted in the ocean of inner secrets, and one's soul perfected and firmly stabilized, so that it becomes a pure mirror that is receptive of the disclosures of the attributes of the Real in their complete perfection. He will recognize his soul as a mirror,

214 Q Naḥl 16:118.
215 Q Dhāriyāt 51:21.

and he will recognize the Real through God's disclosure in his soul. God says, **We will show them our signs in the horizons and in themselves until it becomes clear to them that He is the Real.**[216] The Holy Tradition confirms this meaning upon the tongue of the Beloved ﷺ, wherein God says: "O my servants, it is none other than your deeds that I reckon for you."[217] Their reckoning is their manifestation through their disclosed forms. The Tradition continues, "then I will fulfill them for you" upon the unveiling of those forms. In this world you perform actions and then forget them, while in the next world you will see them. The Tradition continues: "Whoever finds good, let him praise his Lord; and whoever finds other than that, let him blame none other than his soul." The one who finds good praises God because he witnesses the disclosure of the Benefactor (*al-Mun'im*) upon him. The one who finds other than that, meaning ugly forms, should blame none other than his soul.

This Tradition sheds further Light on the hadith, "The one who recognizes himself recognizes his Lord"[218] because the one who recognizes his Lord sees none other than God, for all apart from Him is illusion and ephemerality. Such a person never sees an evil, by virtue of the saying, "All good is between Your hands, and evil does not reach You." The knower of God sees only beauty, and so his recompense is never interrupted. God says, **Save those who believe and perform righteous deeds,**

216 Q Fuṣṣilat 41:53.
217 Muslim, *Ṣaḥīḥ*, 2:1096-1097.
218 Nawawī, *Manthūrāt*, 286.

for theirs shall be a reward unceasing.[219] They have a rightful claim over everything, because they see none other than their own character. So be beautiful, and you will behold existence as being beautiful. The way to attain this is to characterize yourself by the character traits of the Real within your own delimited existence, and in a manner that is worthy of servanthood, until your character traits become purified, your breaths become elevated, and your constitution achieves equilibrium.

For the beauty of the spirit's command (*jamāl al-rūḥ al-amrīya*) cannot be known except in a state of purity. This is why the *Lām* of Constriction is the disclosure-site in which your spirit becomes constricted, and your perishing body is split into two halves, so you can attain the reality of gnosis. For in the *Hā'* you see the Light by virtue of divine mercy. But in the *Lām* of Constriction, only the one who inhabits the spiritual realm can know Him. From there, [the wayfarer] gazes at the physical realm and each day witnesses the reality of, **Whose is the kingdom this Day? It is God's, the One, the Paramount.**[220]

---

219 Q Tīn 95:6.
220 Q Ghāfir 40:16.

22.

The Assumption of Character Traits and the Verification of Truth (*al-Takhalluq wa'l-Taḥaqquq*)

Mudhākara from the Friday
Gathering of 26th Rajab 1436/ 15th May 2015

Bismillāh al-Raḥmān al-Raḥīm

Know, may God adorn your bodily limbs with complete conformity, and bestow upon you the reality of the attributes, that during the previous gatherings we delved deeply into the everlasting presence (*ḥaḍrat al-khulūd*), which is the Garden of the gnostic and his gushing spring of direct witnessing. We spoke about the manner of reconnecting the body to the Light in order for the lover to enter upon the podium of annihilation on the carpet of presence, so that he may pass away from his idol of human nature (*ṣanamuhu al-nāsūtī*) and return to his true luminous nature in the divine Command. Following this night journey of direct tasting, he ascends with his true luminous nature to the source of Light and the quarry of felicity, Sayyidunā Muḥammad ﷺ. And when the servant achieves realization of this witnessing-site, wayfaring becomes easy for him in accordance with what was ordained in pre-eternity, by way of ease and divine wisdom. For when he reaches the All-Encompassing Master (*al-Sayyid al-Jāmiʿ*) ﷺ, he will have received permission both to drink and for the veil to be lifted. He will be granted authorization to directly taste the level of constriction (*martabat al-qabḍ*) wherein the spirits are seized (*tuqbaḍ*) at death, and where all receptacles come to naught completely, to the point that the servant becomes a perfected spirit and a pure inblowing that returns to its Lord pleasing and well pleased. Thereupon, the spirit returns to him with what no eye has seen and no ear has heard. The one who reaches this Muḥammadan wellspring becomes worthy of entering onto the podium of the adoption of the All-Merciful's character traits. It is said that God revealed to Dāwūd ﷺ, "Adopt My character traits, for one of My traits is that I am the Patient."

Thus, when the servant enters into the arena of the adoption of character traits by virtue of constant conformity to the Master of Masters ﷺ, he becomes, as God's Folk say, a Perfect Human Being (*insān kāmil*). The Perfect Human is the one whose attributes of soul have become perfected in all the presences, which are the presences of the divine names, attributes, properties, and acts, such that his act passes away in God's act, witnessing the truth that there is no agent but God, and tasting the meaning of the verse, **God has created you as well as what you do.**[221] Then he passes away in the presence of the

---

221 Q Ṣāffāt 37:96.

attributes, and directly tastes the meaning of the Holy Tradition wherein God says, "I become the hearing by which he hears, the seeing with which he sees, the hand with which he grasps, and the foot by which he walks."[222] After that, he ascends to the podium of annihilation in the Essence, and witnesses with the eye of his heart the meaning of the Prophet's ﷺ words, "The most truthful word that a poet has ever said is the word of Labīd, 'Verily, everything other than God is unreal,'"[223] as well as other verses that point to the proximity of the Lord to the servant. No one can aspire to understand such passages with their intellect, unless they cast their heart down at the doorstep of divine majesty. Having divested himself of his own bankruptcy and separative sense of self, the servant attains the Treasure of the Supreme Intellect. All of this, moreover, is through direct taste and sheer faith in accordance with what was revealed in the Qur'ān, and without any indwelling or unification. It is none other than emulation (*ittibāʿ*) accompanied by divine success (*tawfīq*); servanthood characterized by great exactitude (*tadqīq*); and the fruit of unveiling and truth-verification (*tahqīq*).

So when the servant enters the presence of the Essence by knowledge and witnessing, he is granted direct knowledge of the properties and authorities of all the presences. This is because his direct knowledge of the all-comprehensiveness of the Essence casts him into the knowledge of the multiplicity

222 Bukhārī, *Ṣaḥīḥ*, 2:1319.
223 Muslim, *Ṣaḥīḥ*, 2:975.

of the names and attributes. The names and the attributes are necessarily enfolded within the Essence; do you not see that God says, **He is God, other than whom there is no other god, Knower of the unseen and the seen; He is the Compassionate, the Merciful. He is God, other than whom there is no other god, the Sovereign, the Holy, Peace, the Faithful, the Protector, the Mighty, the Compeller, the Proud. Glory be to Him above the partners they ascribe.**[224] Observe how He points to His Most Beautiful Names after having mentioned the Identity of His unseen Essence. Therefore, when the authority of the Essence comes to manifest, the acts and the attributes disappear through the Essence. Moreover, the authority of the Essence will not manifest until the Day of Resurrection, when each name returns to the authority of His Essence and to the property of its root, and the name-disclosures pass away. What then remains is the authority of the Essence, which subsists as God wills it to subsist, until the eschatological property of the name-disclosure comes to an end.

Ibn Mardūyah and Bayhaqī narrate a hadith the authority of Anas concerning the verse **And the trumpet will be blown, whereupon whosoever is in the heavens and on the earth will swoon, save those whom God wills.**[225] The Prophet ﷺ said: "Among those whom God excludes will be Gabriel, Michael and the Angel of Death. God will say, 'O Angel of Death, who is left?' He will reply, 'What remains is Your Noble Everlasting

224 Q Ḥashr 59:22-23.
225 Q Zumar 39:68.

Face, as well as Your servants Gabriel, Michael, and the Angel of Death.' He will say, 'Give death to the soul of Michael.' Then He will say—and He knows best—'O Angel of Death, who is left?' He will reply, 'What remains is Your Noble Everlasting Face, as well as Your servants Gabriel and the Angel of Death.' He will say, 'Take the soul of Gabriel.' Then He says, and He knows best: 'Who is left O Angel of death?' Then He will say—and He knows best—'O Angel of Death, who is left?' He will reply, 'What remains is Your Noble Everlasting Face, as well as Your servant the Angel of Death, and he is dead.' God will say, 'Die!' Then He will call out, 'I began creation, and now I bring it back! Where are the proud tyrants?' No one will answer Him. Then He will call out, '**Whose is the kingdom this day?**' No one will answer Him. Then He will say, '**It is God's, the One, the Paramount!**' Then the Trumpet will be blown again, and everyone will be resurrected and will see for themselves."[226]

In this world, however, each name remains in the state of its own specificity by manifesting its disclosures of the herebelow. That is because the hereafter possesses the property of the union of separation (*jamʿ al-farq*), as will occur at the return and the gathering of the Muslims, and in fact all nations, under the intercession of al-Muṣṭafā ﷺ. And since he ﷺ is the most perfected creature in his knowledge of his Lord, he is singled out by his specific quality of bringing together multiplicity and separation; for he was granted the all-encompassing words,

---

226 Bayhaqī, *al-Baʿth wa'l-nushūr*, 204.

which is why this master is singled out by this supreme pulpit (*al-minbar al-aʿẓam*), for he is the all-encompassing master and the supreme intermediary who was sent to perfect the noble character traits ﷺ. Thus, his was a universal sending forth to all the worlds, because his receptivity (*qābilīya*) encompasses all receptivities. For he is the Prophet by way of primacy (*bi'l-aṣāla*), and the other Prophets are his vicegerents (*khulafā'*). All nations are his nation, such that all are enfolded under his banner. God says, **And We have not sent you except as a mercy unto the worlds;**[227] and He says, **And we sent not thee except as bearer of glad tidings and a warner to mankind entire, but most of mankind know not;**[228] and He says, **O Prophet, truly We have sent thee as a witness, as a bearer of glad tidings, and as a warner, and as one who calls unto God by His leave, and as a luminous lamp.**[229] Thus, his station is praiseworthy (*maḥmūd*) on every tongue, and his Qur'ān brings together all the revealed Books. He is the exclusive oneness of that totality, and the totality of that exclusive oneness, and he is the one who transforms all character traits into noble ones. This is why one of the greatest manifestation-sites of his mercy, that was sent unto all the worlds, is that the elite proclamation of *tawḥīd* cannot be attained except through him. He is the cause of proximity and divine election.

227 Q Anbiyā' 21:107.
228 Q Saba' 34:28.
229 Q Aḥzāb 33:45-46.

So do not imagine that you can invoke the Prophet's name yet turn away from his Light, and be brought near. Turning away from his Light is the very definition of being distant and cut off. So beware the darkness and its reach. Entering into the elite proclamation of *tawḥīd* requires stripping away all the obstacles which God's folk have broken down into five categories: the lower self (*nafs*), Satan, this world (*dunyā*), caprice (*hawā*), and mankind (*nās*).

As for the verse, **I am God's Messenger unto all of you,**[230] it means that this applies to every genus. This is why the vicegerency of the Messenger ﷺ was with respect to all of mankind by virtue of the finality of His sanctity. Thus, a saint of his community who is upon the nature of Moses ﷺ, or upon the nature of Jesus ﷺ, is not perfected by virtue of the fact that he has not achieved firmness in the other presences. As for the one who is Muḥammadan, he is not delimited at that point by any single presence, time, or place. For he follows the one who was sent to the entirety of man and jinn-kind. This is clear proof that whoever aspires to know God must follow the Master of Creation ﷺ both inwardly and outwardly. For there is no end to witnessing Lordship, and whoever puts his faith in his own ideas, and is not only enticed by his lower self into thinking that he has attained, but also becomes lax with regard to the divine Law, and ceases to seek—such is a deluded servant, imagining that he has reached somewhere, only to find out that it is Hellfire.

---

230 Q A'rāf 7:158.

As for arriving at the Real, it has no end because the Real has no end. And if you wish to assign a beginning and an end to it, then consider its beginning to be unadulterated *tawḥīd*, and its end to be an ascension in one's incapacity to know Him directly. Similarly, the courtesies of servanthood have no end, and the more the servant ascends in direct knowledge and is immersed in the Lights of proximity, the more courtesy he observes in his servanthood. If you find a servant to have been deprived of courtesy, you should know that he is more beast than man.

As for the verse that we mentioned, **And we have not sent thee except as bearer of glad tidings and a warner to mankind entire, but most of mankind know not,**[231] there is a hadith that confirms its meaning. Jābir b. ʿAbd Allāh ﷺ narrated that God's Messenger ﷺ said, "I was given five things which none other was given before me. I have been granted victory through dread for the marching distance of a month; and the earth has been made as a place of prayer and ritually pure and purifying, so that wherever any member of my community may be when it is time to pray, he may pray; and spoils of war have been permitted to me, though they were not to anyone before me; and I have been granted the intercession; and Prophets used to be sent to their people alone, while I was sent to all mankind."[232] There is no need to say more, for the Prophet ﷺ said it all.

God says, **O Prophet, We have sent thee as a witness, and a bearer of glad tidings, and a warner, and a caller to God by**

---

231 Q Sabaʾ 34:28.
232 Bukhārī, *Ṣaḥīḥ*, 1:90.

His leave, and a luminous lamp;[233] that is, "We have sent you forth with the truth as witness," for he is God's witness over creation, and the one who witnesses his Light ﷺ arrives through him to God, as he ﷺ said, "The one who sees me has seen the Real, because Satan cannot take on my form."[234] That is to say, "The one who knows me knows God." What this means is witnessing his Light ﷺ through which the hearts and spirits attain direct knowledge of the Real. This is why the vision of his noble Light is the highest gain and the most precious object of quest according to the gnostics. For he ﷺ is the Illuminating Lamp whose luminous reality was made a lamp by virtue of the disclosure of God's name *al-Nūr*, the Light. This is why the eye of the believer's heart who has tasted true faith is illuminated by his Light. To this effect, Ḥārith said, "I woke up as a true believer."[235] For the Prophet is the radiant sun whose rays shine upon all those who have faith in him and acknowledge his truth.

---

233 Q Aḥzāb 33:45-46.

234 Bukhārī, *Ṣaḥīḥ*, 3:1415.

235 "The holy Prophet asked his companion: 'How have you woken this morning, O Ḥārith?' (*kayfa aṣbaḥta yā Ḥārith*). He responded: 'I woke up as a true believer.' Upon hearing this, the Prophet said: 'Watch what you say! For everything has its true nature, and what is your true nature?' Ḥārith responded: 'My soul has become detached from the world. I fast during the day, and I keep vigil at night. It is as if I see the throne of God on display, and as if I see the inhabitants of the Garden visiting each other, and as if I see the inhabitants of the Fire howling therein.' Upon hearing this, the Prophet said: 'O Ḥārith, you have direct knowledge (*ʿaraft*) so be steadfast.' He repeated it three times." Ṭabarānī, *al-Muʿjam al-kabīr*, 2:266.

Thus, no one can reach the Real except by following in his footsteps. He becomes the imam of a prayer that only ends on the Day of Resurrection: **And those who are constant in their prayers.**[236] And God proclaims the Light of His Beloved ﷺ in the verse, **O people of the Book, Our Messenger has come unto you, making clear to you much of what you once hid of the Book, and pardoning much. There has come unto you from God a Light and a clear Book whereby God guides whosoever seeks His contentment unto the ways of peace, and brings them out of darkness into Light by His leave, and guides them unto a straight path.**[237] In this verse, God makes it clear that the divine command is a Light. The intended meaning here is not the Qur'ān, but rather al-Muṣṭafā ﷺ. This is the precise meaning of **from God a Light.** For his reality is luminous, and that is why he had no shadow and why he could see behind him just as well as he could in front of him. His Light preceded his messengerhood by virtue of the hadith, "[God first created] the Light of your Prophet, O Jābir." It is as though His subtle Light took on the shape of the configuration of the Messenger Sayyidunā Muḥammad ﷺ, just as Gabriel عليه السلام took on the likeness of a flawless human being sent to Maryam, upon her be peace.

There is no difference between the clay's assumption and embodiment in the form of a flawless human being, and the Light's assumption of the form of the Messenger Muḥam-

236 Q Maʿārij 70:23.
237 Q Māʾida 5:15-16.

mad ﷺ. This is the true nature of Sayyidunā Muḥammad ﷺ; he is sheer Light that became dense and was embodied, by God's permission, so that the prophetic form could come to manifest in a specific time as a **mercy unto the worlds.** Then it once again became subtle to the eye when the time of that manifestation came to an end, and he returned to his original state of non-delimited spirit. This does not contradict the fact that he ﷺ was created from clay, for this is his created nature (*khilqa*), while that is his reality (*ḥaqīqa*). There is therefore no contradiction between his spirituality (*rūḥānīya*) and his humanity (*bashariya*). The Light's assumption of a form was sheer mercy, so that the *Kāf* of *Iḥsān* may come to manifest.

You should know also that Light is a pre-eternal attribute that subsists in the exclusive Essence; and through its intermediacy, God brought the heavens and the earth from non-existence into existence, because when Light discloses itself upon a thing or in a thing, it brings it into manifestation. God says, **God is the Light of the heavens and the earth.**[238] Through the intermediacy of this Light, all possible things acquire their ontological and epistemological manifestations. Thus Light in relation to existence is like the spirit in relation to the body. The attribute of Light is the starting point of creation, of existentiation (*ījād*), of manifestation, and of direct knowledge of all possible things.

The Prophet ﷺ said, "The first thing that God created was my Light." From that Light, all lights branch out and all stages

---

238 Q Nūr 24:35.

unfold. The Light mentioned in the verse **God is the Light of the heavens and the earth** is the sheer Light (*al-nūr al-mujarrad*). As for the relative Light that is created and that is expressed by Muḥammad ﷺ, He assigned a likeness to it in the verse, **The likeness of His Light is as a niche.** He ﷺ is the glass of divine love which carries that holy, pure, and pre-eternal Light. As for the reality of divine Light itself, we cannot speak of it in any respect, which is why He compared it to the likeness of it and not to the Light itself, which is the sheer primordial Light. Thus, divine transcendence (*tanzīh*) remains transcendent, and immanence (*tashbīh*) follows transcendence, and all things are enfolded within the core of transcendence. So what a delight his community has in him ﷺ! For through him, the Ummah's all-encompassing circumference becomes the Center.

23.

Each Acts According to His Own Disposition

(*Kullun Ya'mal 'alā Shākilatih*)

Mudhākara from the Friday
Gathering of 3rd Sha'bān 1436/22nd May 2015

Bismillāh al-Raḥmān al-Raḥīm

Know, dear wayfarer, may the Lord grant you success, that God made the realities of the names to be naturally disposed in the innate disposition of the human being through the blessing of the spirit-inblowing. As such, the human being undergoes the effects of the names while still in the secure dwelling place (*qarār makīn*) of the womb. The names, moreover, differ in accordance with the differences of the fate that is ordained for each servant in pre-eternity, whether salvation or damnation. This is why one finds that the name-disclosures and their traces repeatedly exert influence upon the human being. Some of these are manifest and others are hidden. Humans, moreover, incline to the names that disclose themselves in them and that bear an impact upon them. God says, **Verily, God does not**

change what is within a people until they change what is in themselves.[239] The human being therefore cannot change anything around him until the realities that are blown within him are changed.

God's wisdom among His creatures is tremendous, and His blessings are not stripped away from them except on account of their discourtesy. Outward blessings are stripped when a person abandons outward acts of obedience, and inner blessings are stripped when a person abandons self-examination (*murāqaba*), direct witnessing (*mushāhada*), and spiritual struggle (*mujāhada*). God the Just bestows in the measure of the courtesy (*adab*) of the person towards Him, and each station has rights and courtesies. Whoever is remiss with regard to any form of courtesy must quickly repent, and whoever delays the repentance will be deprived. Those who reside in the realm of offense (*isā'a*) should not imagine themselves to be winners. For God only delays, He does not ignore; and this delay is in order to allow us to turn to Him in repentance. When the servant persists in his disobedience, the punishment becomes multiplied. There is no doubt, moreover, that the difference between the punishment of the next world and the punishment of this world is enormous. This is why the disciple must exert efforts to remain amid the Lights (*al-anwār*) and beneath the concealment of the righteous chosen ones (*al-akhyār*). Ibn 'Aṭā' Allāh al-Sakandarī (d. 709/1310) said in his Aphorisms

239 Q Ra'd 13:11.

(*Ḥikam*), "God does not change the Lights of direct witnessing and of eye-witnessing that are within people's hearts unless they exchange their beautiful courtesy for discourtesy." Thus, if a person is mindful of courtesy and is sincere, the doors of the Elect are open for him.

This is why the spiritual struggle begins from within you by binding your thoughts according to the standards of al-Muṣṭafā ﷺ, so that states of conformity are generated from them. The saint may reach a station where he is cloaked with the mantle of divine protection and the robe of success and providence. He may even hear the incoming thoughts in the form of a trial telling him, "do whatever you wish, for I have forgiven you." This was the distinction by which God singled out the people of the battle of Badr, may God be pleased with all of them. But this trial may only be given to those who have completely ridden themselves of disobedience, and adorn themselves with obedience in every breath, and who enter into the witnessing-site of the verse, **Everything is from God.**[240]

God may change the heart of one of His servants in order to test them. He may strip them of interaction (*muʿāmala*) or of direct knowledge (*maʿrifa*), for He is the one who fluctuates the hearts of His servants however He wishes. If the servant never experiences fright or terror, he will remain in the darkness of alterity and forget God, so God will cause him to forget his own soul; **And when God desires evil for a people, there**

240 Q Nisāʾ 4:78.

is no repelling it.[241] We ask God for safety through His gratuitous favor and generosity.

It is God who manifests the lightning of direct witnessing (*barq al-mushāhada*) to whichever servant He wishes, so that the servant may gaze upon the Holy Presence. The one who reveres the celestial steed of divine providence (*burāq al-ʿināya*) enters and receives the glad tiding of divine mercy. As for the one who regards what comes to him from his Lord and considers the lightning to be merely flickering light, this is a sign of depravation which will lead to regret.

Know that when someone gazes upon the Holy Presence, His Lord will send him Lights in a successive manner, so that he is not overcome by a spiritual state and so that he finds intimacy in them gradually. And in order for him to attain a station of firmness, the Lights do not leave him night or day, whether he closes his eyes or opens them. The flashes of Light continue to display themselves before him until the Lights of the face-to-face encounter (*muwājaha*) disclose themselves to him. These are the Lights that encounter him with their flashes, causing him to fall into a state of dazzled indifference toward everything other-than-God, and he sees nothing but God.

Know also that the Lights of this face-to-face encounter are what produce the clouds of mystical inrushes (*saḥāb al-wāridāt*) and the rainclouds that herald the descent of bestowals from the sky of disclosures. Do you not see how the monk Baḥīra turned

---

241 Q Raʿd 13:11.

himself in his entirety toward God's Messenger ﷺ when he saw the raincloud of glad tidings giving him shade? For the thin white cloud (*ghamām*) conceals the spirit. Thus, this cloud that is formed from the Lights of the encounter is filled with sciences and innermost secrets, and sends forth thunderbolts (*ṣawāʾiq*) so that your sensory realm is seized from you. Through it, the breast of the one who is engulfed by divine providence is rent asunder. As for the people who deny, they are at a lowly station. They deny these Lights and remain in the distance of their own illusions without being aware of it, oblivious in the gloom of their sense perceptions.

This is why the act of thinking well of God (*ḥusn al-ẓann biʾLlāh*) necessitates the recurrence of the inrushes of Light. For it has been transmitted that on the authority of Abū Hurayra ﷺ, that the Prophet ﷺ said that God says "I am as My servant thinks of Me, and I am with him when he remembers Me. If he remembers Me to himself, I remember him within Myself. If he invokes Me in an assembly, I invoke him in a better assembly. If he draws near unto Me by a hand span, I draw near unto him by an arm's length. If he draws near unto Me by an arm's length, I draw near unto him by a cubit. If he comes to Me walking, I go to him running."[242]

So gnosis is the sign of thinking well of God. However, if you do not think well of your Lord, that is a sign of your ignorance and obliviousness. For you to commit grave sins would

---

242 Bukhārī, *Ṣaḥīḥ*, 3:1494.

be less severe in God's eyes than for you to say something about God of which you have no knowledge. Thus the one who has no Light in his heart, yet speaks about the presence of Lights, would better remain silent, for this is the very definition of discourtesy. As for the one whose heart is filled with Lights, let him then speak of God's blessings: **As for your Lord's blessings, speak of them.**[243]

As for the one whose heart is darkness upon darkness, yet he speaks of direct tasting, through his words he distances people from the presence of the Real and bars them from God's Path. And he carries the burdens of the sins of the ones whom he conceals from the Light of the Real, for his words cause people to think poorly of the God's Path. **And that He may punish the hypocritical men and women, and the idolatrous men and the idolatrous women, who think an evil thought concerning God. Upon them is an evil turn. God is wroth with them, curses them, and prepares Hell for them—what an evil journey's end.**[244] The evil turn (*dā'ira al-saw'*) is the eclipse of darkness, and it is the fate of the one who thinks poorly of the Lord of the Worlds, which includes thinking poorly of the Prophet ﷺ, his companions, or the saints.

Thus, if you think well of the Lord of the Worlds, you will always find Him to be as you think of Him. And the one who thinks well of God, His Prophets, His friends, and in fact all of His creation, such is the one who has adopted the character

243 Q Ḍuḥā 93:11.
244 Q Fatḥ 48:6.

traits of the All-Merciful. As for the one who holds in his heart rancor, hate, and grudges, how could the camel of his lower self pass through the eye of the needle of the dot of knowledge, which only opens when it is revered (*ta'ẓīm*)? This dot is Sayyidunā 'Alī, may God ennoble his countenance. And the one who does not see the beauty of the Real in the smallest thing, and does not comprehend that, let him remember constantly that he will see everything that he has done in his life from the day of his birth to the day of his death, on one single scroll. This is why you must train yourself to experience amplitude in constraint, and to witness the great in the smallest thing.

24.

The Exclusive Oneness of the All
and the Allness of Exclusive Oneness
(*Majmūʿ al-Aḥadīya wa-Aḥadīyat al-Jumūʿ*)

Mudhākara from the Friday
Gathering of 10th Shaʿbān 1436/29th May 2015

Bismillāh al-Raḥmān al-Raḥīm

Know, may God embrace your heart with His Lights, that the secret of union (*al-jamʿ*) and its inner dimension is an expression of the totality of the divine names. In other words, the secret of the *Hāʾ* is the sum total of the names which are differentiated by their wellsprings and drinking-places. The drinking-place of the All-Hearing (*Samīʿ*), for instance, is not the same as the drinking-place of the Speaking (*Mutakallim*). These names are exclusive as far as their Essence is concerned, but have differing drinking-places with respect to the disclosures and the attributes. The knowers of God, in all their variety, each gaze upon the Essence from the vantage point of a specific drinking-place of a divine name. This is what the people of realization call *majmūʿ al-aḥadīya*, the allness of exclu-

249

sive oneness. In our Order, more specifically, we call this the Hidden *Alif*. Note that there is a difference between saying "the exclusive oneness of the all" and "the allness of exclusive oneness." There is a vast difference between the two terms, which is known to those who are fit to know it. It is not a mere switching of terms. If God wills that we live long enough to do it, we shall read the *Hā'* from the perspective of the exclusive oneness of the all, showing how each differs from the other in seventy principal ways.

To clarify this further, the disclosure of the *Hā'* of the Hidden *Alif* corresponds to the one who witnesses the forms of reality in their exact detail. That is, he knows that each form harks back to the all-comprehensive reality: **And to Him returns the entire affair.**[245] However, such a witnesser gazes upon the second separation (*al-farq thānī*) inasmuch as his own preparedness enables him to do so. This is why in our Order we enter the disciple upon the *Hā'* of the Name, because that is closest to his preparedness. Therein, he learns the pure meaning of the absolute within the delimited (*al-iṭlāq fī'l-taqyīd*), and through the *Hā'* he learns the *tawḥīd* of union (*tawḥīd al-jam'*).[246] Then he begins his wayfaring level by level until he comes to recognize the difference between one name and another, and one attribute and another, until he finally arrives at the Hidden *Alif*.

245 Q Hūd 11:123.
246 The Shaykh refers to the "*tawḥīd* of union" as the first secret that the disciple learns on the Path, followed by the second secret which is called the "*tawḥīd* of separation" (*tawḥīd al-farq*).

All of this, moreover, is through the door of the allness of exclusive oneness (*majmūʿ al-aḥadīya*), such that he witnesses the varieties of each name and their specific qualities, and he traces each of them back to the single Essence. The disciple is like someone who regards the forms of mankind in all their variety while knowing that they share a common root that unites all of them, a root from which they all sprang forth and branched out, a root which is none other than Adam ﷺ. The Master of Mankind ﷺ said, "O mankind, your Lord is one, and your father is one. All of you are from Adam, and Adam is from dust. The noblest of you in God's sight is the most Godfearing of you. No Arab has any superiority over any non-Arab, except through Godfearing. Have I not conveyed? O God, bear witness!"[247]

Now, the one who drinks from this wellspring cannot remain with the all-comprehensive source because of the dominance of the authority of separation over him. But this separation is luminous, not dark; it is exactly like the Light which has no color, but takes on the color of the Niche. Thus, the one who beholds the differences in the Lights with regard to their colors, and traces each color back to its luminous source where there is no color—such a person is in the allness of exclusive oneness, because he gazes upon union through the eye of separation.

As for the disclosure of the exclusive oneness of the all (*aḥadīyat al-jumū'*), this is like the one who sees these forms

---

247 Aḥmad, *Musnad*, 5:411.

through the very reality of the human being, and does not turn his gaze to anything other than that reality. This witnesser cannot differentiate between one drinking-place and another, nor between one name and another, until he perfects the seven readings of the divine Name. The one who stands at this drinking-place does not see anything of the forms except for their exclusive oneness (*aḥadīya*), which is the Adamic reality. The people of this type of allness (*majmūʿ*) are distinguished by non-manifest disclosure (*tajallī bāṭinī*), which is the returning-place of all the various names through which He discloses. The realization of this tasting occurs in the presence of the *Lām*, which is the disclosure-site of the Perfect Man.

This witnesser sees no one except for the reality of al-Muṣṭafā ﷺ, and he sees all things as being from his reality; for he is the spring from which those who are brought near drink. God says, **A spring whence drink those brought near.**[248] Those brought near are the ones about whom it is said, "Do not return them back to their castles." Similarly, the one brought near in the Path is the one who sees the mystical glimmer (*lamḥa*) and is mindful of it, and receives an increase in all that is good; not the one who sees it and then withdraws. So if you lose the Light, then take account of your soul and look at what you have done.

Know, moreover, that the incoming thoughts of the lower self are among the grave sins of the spirit. Likewise, when a

---

248 Q Muṭaffifīn 83:28.

divine gift distracts you, it is an obstacle for the spirit. Those brought near remain in the all-comprehensive disclosure (*al-ta-jallī al-jamʿī*), even though they have not left their castles and even though they remain with their wives who are daughters of this world. Those brought near are united with each one of the people of the all-comprehensive disclosure, and they witness the Real in all forms of belief by virtue of the secrets that they have received. They stand in contrast to those who are told to return to their castles (*quṣūr*), which itself is a proof of their deficient (*quṣūr*) knowledge and witnessing. Since the latter's inner-union is too narrow to witness that esoteric reality, they were unreceptive of it when it was unveiled for them. Thus they were ordered to be returned back to their castles due to their deficient comprehension of that esoteric reality.

This is similar to what occurs to the disciples in this world. Some of them attained a station of gnosis, then the esoteric reality of what they have attain becomes manifest to them, but they do not comprehend what they were given from God. So they flee from the Path and are unable to complete the journey. The tongue of their spiritual state in this world is similar to the verbal tongue of those on the Day of Resurrection who, when God discloses Himself to them, will cry, "We seek refuge in God from You!"[249]

Therefore, only those who are patient can attain direct knowledge of God. And if you do not possess direct knowledge

---

249 Muslim, *Ṣaḥīḥ*, 183.

of Him in the herebelow, you will not have direct knowledge of Him in the hereafter. The disciples who are incapable of bearing the esoteric truth (*ḥaqīqa*) are addressed by the Presence on the tongue of divine power: "Return them to their castles, wherein lie the nonexistent forms."

The difference between those who wander aimlessly in the waves of separation and do not cut across the ocean of union, will become clearly manifest on the Day of Resurrection, and the drinking place of each person will become manifest to them. As for the people of the all-comprehensive name-disclosure (*al-tajallī al-jamʿī al-asmāʾī*), they are the perfected elite, and it is they who witness of the Lord of Beauty and Majesty. Tirmidhī narrates, on the authority of Saʿīd b. al-Musayyab, that he met Abū Hurayra who said, "I ask God to unite us in the market of Paradise." Saʿīd said, "Is there a market in Paradise?" He said, "'Yes, the blessed Messenger of God told me that when the people enter Paradise, they shall take up residence in accordance with their deeds. They will be given permission to visit their Lord for the length of a Friday from the days of this world. He will show them His throne and display Himself to them in one of the gardens of Paradise. Pulpits of Light shall be erected for them, as well as pulpits of pearl, pulpits of ruby, pulpits of peridots, pulpits of gold, and pulpits of silver. The lowest of them—although none of them are low—will sit upon a dune of musk and camphor, and they will not regard those sitting upon chairs as having a better seating than them. Abū Hurayra said: "I said: 'O Messenger of God, will we see our Lord?' He said: 'Yes. Do you doubt seeing the sun or the moon on a night when it is full?' We said: 'No.' He said: 'Likewise, you will have no doubt concerning the vision of your Lord. No person shall remain in that gathering except that God will have conversed with him. He will even say to one of them: 'O so-and-so son of so-and-so, do you remember the day when you said such-and-such.' He will remind him of some of his betrayals in this world, whereupon the man will say: "My Lord, did you not forgive me?" He will say: 'Indeed! It is by the vastness of My Forgiveness that you have attained this station of yours.' As they are engaged in this [communion with God], they will be covered by a cloud that will rain upon them a perfume the likes of which they had never smelled before. Our Lord shall say: 'Arise to the generous gifts that I have prepared for you and take whatever you desire.' Then we shall arrive at a market surrounded by angels. Therein shall be what no eye has seen, no ear has heard, and no heart has imagined. Whatever we desire will be carried for us, for nothing therein is bought or sold. In that market, the people of Paradise will meet each other.' He said: 'A person of high rank will meet another of lower rank—and none among them is low—and will be impressed by the clothes that he sees upon him. Their conversation shall not come to an end until [the person of lower standing] shall imagine himself to be wearing something more beautiful than [the former's clothes], because it is not fitting for anyone to feel sadness therein. Then we will return to our dwellings and our wives shall greet us saying: 'Hello and welcome! You are back, and your beauty is even greater than it was before you left.' He will say: 'Today we sat with our Lord, the All-Dominating, His glory extolled! It is fitting that we should return with this [increase in beauty].'"[250]

Know that even though the disclosure of union is one, it manifests for the people of the cosmic levels in accordance with their own levels. This is why there is a variety of pulpits of Light and of pearls and of silver in the hadith. The hadith contains indescribable divine mercy and generosity, in the sense that if it were a disclosure of the exclusive oneness of the all, then no one would see it, but He discloses Himself through the all-ness of exclusive oneness.

In the realm of religious accountability (*taklīf*), servants need a guide who directs the souls to the presence of the All-Holy, and that is none other than wayfaring by means of the Shaykh's own saintly aspiration, which is the paradisal talisman of the Kawthar-Opening (*ṭalsam kawthar al-fatḥ*) by which the disciple ascends to the sapiential arena of the divine names, where the innermost secret of the verse **God taught Adam all the names**[251] becomes manifest.

250 Tirmidhī, *Sunan*, 2:974.
251 Q Baqara 2:31.

Conclusion

It is time to restrain the reins of our pen, for if we were to let it run freely, it would make rounds that this station cannot bear. Our aim is to guide the wayfarer toward the everlasting spiritual breezes and fragrances of witnessing at the presence of the Hidden *Alif*. The latter, for its part, is one of the disclosure-sites of the Singular *Alif* that cannot be encompassed by words or attained through allusion, for it is determined through an imaginal form in the *Hā'*-sphere. God says: **And for the moon, We have decreed mansions, till it returns like an old palm stalk.**[252]

You should know, dear sincere disciple and seeker of the truth, that this book consists of luminous spindrifts that flow forth from the Hidden *Alif* within the delimitation of the *Hā'*. Its purpose is to approximate transcendent meanings to the perishing servant who is searching for pure water to quench his thirst and satisfy his craving. Nonetheless, spiritual meanings of the holy disclosures are only taken from the hearts of men, not from poems or books. We have pointed to you the Path, and it

[252] Q Yā Sīn 36:39.

is up to you to search for one who will take you by the hand in order to extract its treasures.

The *Alif* consists of a sun between two moons—a sun that never sets, and two moons that are the sovereignty of its rays. The spiritual guides are its kernel; they direct others to its norms, and establish its principles. Their inner state is a sun, and their outer states are moons. This is why discourse at this station occurs through symbols which can only be understood by those who abstain from alterity and become a treasure.

Works Cited

1. Abū Dāwūd, al-Sijistānī. *Sunan Abī Dāwūd.* Cairo: Thesaurus Islamicus, 2018.

2. Al-ʿAjlūnī, Ismāʿīl b. Muḥammad. *Kashf al-khafā wa-muzīl al-il-bās ʿammā ishtahara min al-aḥādīth ʿalā alsinat al-nās.* Edited by Aḥmad al-Qallāsh. Beirut: Muʾassasat al-Risāla, 2000.

3. Al-Albānī, Muḥammad Nāṣir al-Dīn. *Silsilat al-aḥādīth al-ṣaḥīḥa wa-shayʾ min fiqhihā.* Riyadh: Dār al-Maʿārif, n.d.

4. Al-ʿAsqalānī, Ibn Ḥajar. *Fatḥ al-Bārī bi-sharḥ Ṣaḥīḥ al-Bukhārī.* Edited by Muḥibb al-Dīn al-Khaṭīb. Cairo: al-Maktaba al-Salafīya, 1987.

5. Al-Bayhaqī, Aḥmad b. al-Ḥusayn. *al-Baʿth waʾl-nushūr.* Edited by Abū ʿĀṣim al-Shawāmī al-Atharī. Riyadh: Dār al-Ḥajjār, 2015.

6. __________. *Shuʿab al-Imān.* Edited by ʿAbd al-ʿAlī Ashraf ʿAlī. Mumbai: Maktabat al-Rushd, 2003.

7. __________. *Dalāʾil al-nubūwa.* Edited by ʿAbd al-Muʿṭī al-Qalʿajī. Cairo: Dār al-Rayyān, 1988.

8. Al-Bukhārī, Muḥammad b. Ismāʿīl. *Ṣaḥīḥ al-Bukhārī.* Cairo: Thesaurus Islamicus, 2018.

9. __________. *Al-Tārīkh al-kabīr.* Edited by Hāshim al-Nadwī. Hayderabad: Dāʾirat al-maʿārif al-ʿuthmānīya, 1941.

10. Chiabott, Francesco. "Ethique et theologie: la pratique de l'adab dans le traite sur les Noms divins d'Abū l-Qāsim ʿAbd al-Karīm al-Qushayrī (*al-Taḥbīr fī ʿilm al-tadhkīr*)." In *Ethics and Spirituality in Islam: Sufi Adab,* edited by Francesco Chiabotti et al., 165–197. Leiden: Brill.

11. Al-Ḥākim, Muḥammad b. ʿAbd Allāh. *al-Mustadrak ʿalā al-ṣaḥīḥayn*. Cairo: Dār al-Ḥaramayn li'l-Ṭibāʿa wa'l-Nashr, 1997.

12. Ibn Abī ʿĀṣim, Abū Bakr Aḥmad. *Al-Sunna*. Edited by Bāsim b. Faysal al-Jawābira. Riyadh: Dār al-Ṣumayʿī, 1998.

13. Ibn Abī Shaybah, ʿAbd Allah b. Muḥammad. *al-Muṣannaf*. Edited by Ḥamad al-Jumʿa and Muḥammad al-Liḥidān. Riyadh: Maktabat al-Rushd, 2004.

14. Ibn al-Jarrāḥ, Wakīʿ. *Kitāb al-zuhd*. Edited ʿAbd al-Wakīl ʿAbd al-Jabbār al-Faryawānī. Medina: Maktabat al-Dār, 1984.

15. Ibn al-Tamīmī, Ismāʿīl b. Muḥammad. *Musnad Abū Yaʿlā al-Mawṣilī*. Edited by Ḥusayn Salīm Asad. Damascus: Dār al-Thaqāfa al-ʿArabīya, 1993.

16. Ibn Anas, Mālik. *al-Muwaṭṭaʾ*. Cairo: Thesaurus Islamicus, 2018.

17. Ibn ʿAsākir, ʿAlī b. al-Ḥasan. *Tārikh madīnat Dimashq*. Edited by Mūḥibb al-Dīn al-ʿAmrawī. Beirut: Dār al-Fikr, 1995.

18. Ibn Ḥanbal, Aḥmad. *al-Musnad*. Edited by Aḥmad al-Bannā. Beirut: Dār Iḥyāʾ al-Turāth al-ʿArabī, n.d.

19. Ibn Ḥibbān, Muḥammad. *Ṣaḥīḥ Ibn Ḥibbān bi-tartīb Ibn Balbān*. Edited by Shuʿayb al-Arnaʾūṭ. Beirut: Muʾassasat al-Risāla, 1993.

20. Ibn Mājah, Muḥammad b. Yazīd al-Qazwīnī. *Sunan Ibn Mājah*. Edited by Muḥammad Fuʾād al-Bāqī. Cairo: Dār Iḥyāʾ al-Kitāb al-ʿArabī, 1953.

21. Al-Isbahānī, Aḥmad b. ʿAbd Allāh. *Ḥilyat al-awliyāʾ wa-ṭabaqāt al-aṣfiyāʾ*. Beirut: Dār al-Kutub al-ʿIlmīya, 2002.

22. Muslim, Ibn al-Ḥajjāj. *Ṣaḥīḥ Muslim*. Cairo: Thesaurus Islamicus, 2018.

23. Nasr, Seyyed Hossein (editor-in-chief). *The Study Quran: A New Translation with Notes and Commentary*. Edited by Caner Dagli, Maria Massi Dakake, Joseph Lumbard (general editors); Mohammed Rustom (assistant editor). New York: HarperOne, 2015.

24. Al-Nawawī, Yaḥyā b. Sharaf al-Dīn. *al-Manthūrāt wa-ʿuyūn al-masāʾil al-muhimmāt*. Cairo: Dār al-Kutub al-Islāmīya, 1982.

25. Al-Qushayrī, Abū l-Qāsim. *al-Risāla al-Qushayrīya*. Edited by ʿAbd al-Ḥalīm Maḥmūd. Damascus: Dār al-Fikr, 2003.

26. Al-Ṣāliḥī, Muḥammad b. Yusuf. *Subul al-rashād fī sīrat khayr al-ʿibād*. Edited by Muṣṭafā ʿAbd al-Aḥad. Cairo: Lajnat Iḥyāʾ al-Turāth, 1997.

27. Al-Suyūṭī, Jalāl al-Dīn. *Iḥyāʾ faḍāʾil Ahl al-Bayt*. Cairo: Dār al-Marʿārif, 1999.

28. Al-Ṭabarānī, Sulaymān b. Aḥmad. *Al-Muʿjam al-kabīr*. Edited by Ḥamdī ʿAbd al-Majīd al-Salafī. Cairo: Maktabat Ibn Taymīya, 2008.

29. __________. *Al-Muʿjam al-awsaṭ*. Edited by Ṭāriq b. Muḥammad and ʿAbd al-Muḥsin al-Ḥusaynī. Cairo: Dār al-Ḥaramayn, 1995.

30. Al-Ṭabari, Muḥammad b. Jarīr. *Jāmiʿ al-Bayyān ʿan taʾwīl āy al-Qurʾān*. Cairo: Maṭbaʿat Muṣṭafā al-Bābī al-Ḥalabī wa-Awlādih, 1968.

31. Al-Tirmidhī, Abū ʿĪsā. *Sunan al-Tirmidhī*. Cairo: Thesaurus Islamicus, 2018.

32. Al-Zurqānī, Muḥammad ʿAbd al-Bāqī. *Mukhtaṣar al-maqāṣid al-ḥasana fī bayan al-aḥādīth al-mushtahara ʿalā l-alsina*. Edited by Muḥammad al-Ṣabbāgh. Beirut: al-Maktab al-Islāmī, 1982.

Index of Names & Terms

A

Abū Hurayra 22, 35, 137, 152, 196, 198, 215, 216, 245, 254.

Ādam 20, 22, 24, 42, 53, 54, 56, 57, 58, 59, 60, 62, 67, 69, 137, 148, 172, 177, 180, 196, 202, 209, 215, 216, 217, 218, 219, 251, 256.

Aḥmad b. ʿAlīwa/Aḥmad al-ʿAlawī 23, 62, 125.

Algerian 151.

ʿAlī 26, 58, 98, 136, 159, 161, 181, 247.

Alif 14, 17, 18, 19, 22, 24, 67, 87, 88, 89, 114, 119, 125, 130, 134, 135, 136, 141, 147, 154, 155, 160, 168, 177, 189, 257, 258.

Alif, Hidden (*al-Alif al-muqaddar*) 17, 24, 29, 30, 45, 54, 74, 78, 88, 89, 93, 120, 122, 129, 137, 146, 151, 153, 160, 163, 169, 180, 188, 189, 203, 250.

Alif of Exclusive Unity/ Singular *Alif* (*al-Alif al-aḥadī*) 119, 120, 121, 123.

Alif, Primordial/Original (*al-Alif al-aṣlī*) 24, 88, 168, 179, 188.

B

Basmala 135, 136, 159.

Branches of faith (*shuʿab al-īmān*) 154, 155, 157, 161, 169.

Breezes (*nafaḥāt*) 46, 145, 257.

Burāq (celestial steed) 166.

C

City of Knowledge 26.

D

Dāwūd (David) 69, 230.

Day of Increase (*yawm al-mazīd*) 113, 137.

Day of ʿArafa 133, 197.

Demonic counterpart/ comrade (*qarīn*) 166, 201, 210.

Diḥya al-Kalbī 75.

Disclosure-site (*majlā*) 30, 55, 79, 88, 94, 100, 228, 252.

Disclosure (*tajallī*) 26, 37, 44, 55, 70, 99, 100, 101, 111, 112, 119, 122, 131, 156, 197, 227, 232, 237, 250, 251, 252, 253, 254, 256, 257.

Divan/registry (*dīwān*) 61, 172.

Dot, I am the (*anā al-nuqṭa*) 136, 146, 159.

E

Egyptian, the (*qibṭī*) 21.

Everlasting Presence/ Station (*ḥaḍrat/ḥaḍrat al-khulūd*) 14, 24, 163, 165, 171.

Evil eye 201, 210, 211.

Eye-witnessing (*ʿiyān*) 56, 243.

F

False idol (*ṭāghūt*) 34.

Flash (*bāriqa*) 224, 244.

Footstool (*kursī*) 93, 99.

G

Gabriel 20, 52, 75, 80, 83, 94, 112, 114, 208, 232, 233, 238.

Glad harbingers (*mu-bashshirāt*) 103, 104.

Gleam (*lāmiʿa*) 26, 154, 224.

Glimmer (*lamḥa*) 69, 70, 73, 224, 252.

God-given science (*ʿilm ladunnī*) 25.

H

Handful of Light/Lumi-nous Handful (*qabḍa nūrānīya*) 34, 54, 60, 100, 153.

Ḥārith 237.

Ḥasan b. ʿAlī, al- 19.

Hāʾ-center 189.

Hāʾ of Identity (*hāʾ al-huwiyya*) 18, 120, 164, 167.

Hā'-reading (*qirā'a hā'iyya*) 17, 50, 89.

I

Iblīs 33, 34, 83, 84, 109, 177, 218, 219.

Ibn Mas'ūd, 'Abdullāh 20, 105.

Ibn 'Abbās, 'Abdullah (b. 'Abbās) 25, 49, 62, 64, 72, 175, 181, 195, 212.

Ibn 'Aṭā' Allāh al-Iskandarī 120, 242.

Imaginal faculty (*khayāl*) 39.

Inerrancy (*'iṣma*) 55, 89, 93.

Innate disposition (*fiṭra*) 94, 127, 139, 217, 241.

Inner vision (*baṣīra*) 32, 55, 56, 70, 88, 108, 153, 164, 173, 174, 177, 178, 180, 188, 198, 224.

Inrush (*wārid*) 45, 107, 125, 244, 245.

Intellect, Muḥammadan (*al-'aql al-Muḥammadī*) 27.

Intellect, Supreme (*al-'aql al-akbar*) 21, 24, 25, 29, 30, 231.

Intermediary (*wāsiṭa*) 47, 54, 63, 64, 68, 75, 80, 174, 234.

J

Jābir 53, 197, 212, 236, 238.

Jesus/Īsā/Son of Mary 24, 43, 62, 68, 81, 85, 100, 101, 194, 235, 261.

Jinn 32, 40, 178, 185, 201, 235.

K

Kāf of Immanence/*Kāf* of Iḥsān (*kāf al-tashbīh*) 31, 156, 194, 239.

Kawthar 165, 256.

Ka'ba 195, 212, 217.

Khiḍr, al- 25, 87.

L

Labīd 211.

Lām of Constriction (*lām al-qabḍ*) 17, 18, 89, 120, 121, 160, 168, 169, 179, 188, 203, 216, 228.

Lām of Gnosis (*lām al-ma'rifa*) 17, 18, 120, 121, 168, 179, 188, 203.

Lote Tree 99, 100, 166.

M

Mālik, Imām 133.

Means of approach (*wasīla*) 174.

Michael 20, 232, 233.

Mīm 33, 157.

Moses 20, 21, 24, 25, 87, 108, 111, 184, 185, 196, 203, 235.

Muḥammadan Reality 47, 62, 63, 65, 81, 88.

N

Name, Hidden (*al-ism al-maknūn*) 58.

Name, singular (*al-ism al-mufrad*) 125, 134, 136, 137, 155, 169.

Norm(s), divine (sing. *Nāmūs*) 24, 25, 83, 84, 85, 113, 165, 187, 258.

Numerology 155.

Nūn 155, 156.

P

Perfect Man/Human Being (*al-insān al-kāmil*) 23, 39, 40, 54, 56, 57, 58, 59, 60, 61, 62, 69, 70, 73, 75, 76, 88, 96, 100, 108, 128, 166, 172, 187, 199, 209, 210, 216, 238, 241, 242, 252.

Perfect servant (*al-'abd al-kāmil*) 183.

Pole (*quṭb*) 61.

Presence, Sanctified (*ḥaḍrat al-quds*) 40, 41, 45.

Q

Qatāda 19.

Qibla 18, 49, 212, 217.

R

Raphael 20.

Rare readings (*qirā'at shādhdha*) 80, 136.

Realm, Invincible (*jabarūt*) 39, 40, 59, 73, 74, 172, 183.

Realm, Sensory/Physical (*mulk*) 24, 39, 68, 75, 122, 128, 129, 167, 170, 172, 173, 174, 177, 180, 188, 189, 190, 208, 228, 245.

Realm, Spiritual (*ma-lakūt*) 39, 40, 59, 70, 73, 74, 120, 122, 128, 132, 167, 170, 172, 183, 188, 189, 228.

Renewer (*mujaddid*) 65, 195.

Retreat (*khalwa*) 206.

Reviver-saint 195.

Roaming, pious (*siyāḥa*) 32, 165.

S

Seal (*khatm*) 22, 52, 65, 67, 68, 81, 88, 195.

Second Coming 24.

Separation (*farq*) 19, 40, 59, 60, 81, 87, 88, 119, 199, 200, 201, 209, 224, 225, 233, 250, 251, 254.

Soul, Perfected (*nafs kāmila*) 39, 42.

Soul, Pleasing (*nafs al-rāḍiya*) 21.

Soul(s), partial (*nufūs juzʾiya*) 39, 42.

Spiritual excellence (*iḥsān*) 83, 113, 142, 157, 195.

Subtle grace (pl. *raqāʾiq*) 18, 32.

Sunnah 44, 117, 187.

Supreme, Name (*al-ism al-aʿzam*) 58, 68, 88.

T

Tablet (*lawḥ*) 74, 79, 122, 164, 171, 172, 225.

Talisman (*ruqya*) 84, 201, 210.

Tasting, direct (*dhawq*) 13, 50, 56, 78, 83, 110, 112, 114, 146, 194, 224, 229, 230, 231, 246.

Throne-status (*ʿarshīya*) 108.

Training, spiritual (*tar-biya*) 23, 71, 174.

Triangle 136, 200.

U

Union (*jamʿ*) 19, 40, 60, 119, 123, 173, 199, 201, 209, 219, 224, 225, 233, 249, 250, 251, 253, 254, 256.

V

Vicegerency (*khilāfa*) 42, 52, 57, 58, 62, 63, 88, 196, 217, 235.

Voice, disembodied (sing. *hātif*) 190.

W

Whisper, demonic 210.

Whisper, obsessive (*was-wasa*) 201, 210, 212.

White days (*al-ayyām al-bīḍ*) 199.

Witnessing, direct (*shu-hūd*) 13, 56, 77, 106, 142, 154, 167, 180, 213, 219, 220, 223, 224, 229, 242, 243, 244.

Z

Zaynab 51.

Printed and bound
in the United States of America